Rainbow of Hope

Rainbow of Hope
True Courage in Crisis

April Lynne Marshall

gatekeeper press

Columbus, Ohio

Rainbow of Hope: True Courage in Crisis

Published by Gatekeeper Press
2167 Stringtown Rd, Suite 109
Columbus, OH 43123-2989
www.GatekeeperPress.com

The editorial work for this book is entirely the product of the author. Gatekeeper Press did not participate in and is not responsible for any aspect of this element.

Library of Congress Control Number: 2020943190

ISBN (hardcover): 9781662903403
ISBN (paperback): 9781662903410
eISBN: 9781662903427

Contents

CHAPTER ONE

Bold Challenge

All at once the entire world changed and people around the globe were beginning to experience what those with mental illness had to negotiate on a regular basis. The novel coronavirus induced a level of anxiety, panic, fear and depression unlike anything in modern civilization. We did not even have time to go through the normal stages of grief as the everyday things and common routines abruptly disappeared. All events were cancelled, colleges, universities, public schools and churches closed down, businesses were vacant, the stock market plummeted, social distancing became the mode of operation and economic recession began in a period of a few days. Some began working from home, but many would just lose their income. Things became traumatic very quickly as the United States watched Italy, France, Spain, England and India go into total lockdown from Covid-19.

How would Americans respond to this unprecedented global pandemic? Would we rally together in generosity and compassion for those most vulnerable or regress into a self-preserving, survival of the fittest mentality? The early stages of behavior were far from encouraging as people began hoarding toilet paper, sanitary items and disinfectants. Grocery stores had to limit purchases of essential items and then limit the number of people shopping. Young people continued to over occupy beaches and bars for spring break, ignoring CDC recommendations for avoiding crowds to reduce contamination. Social media was flooded with misinformation, conspiracy theories and political posturing. After all, the crisis was unfolding the midst of a volatile election year.

By the time the 45th president spoke from the oval office on March 11, 2020, the situation was already an international catastrophe. In fairness, the nation was gripped in shock. There was no transitional period to adjust so our individual and group coping skills were immediately tested. Logically, we all endured a shared sense of loss because the conveniences of life had dissipated with little notice. Now we were left with a myriad of emotions like denial, anger, bargaining, sadness and reluctant acceptance all at the same time. However, the spark of resiliency and contingency planning was becoming more prevalent. Educators moved quickly to on-line learning formats, arrangements were made for children to have school lunches and senior living facilities enforced diligent policies to protect residents.

By the beginning of spring, New York, California and Illinois became the first at restricted people from leaving their homes and other states followed suit. Some municipalities began implementing curfews in an effort to contain the coronavirus. Florida's governor failed to respond to the pandemic until finally imposing a statewide stay-at-home order on April 2, 2020. By that time, the number of positive cases had increased exponentially and the Sunshine State ranked 6th in the United States for the total number of residents suffering from Covid-19. Two days later, there was a federal recommendation that everyone should wear cloth masks when going out in public.

Orlando was America's top destination for tourists and Disney, Universal Studios and Sea World had discontinued operations in mid-March, while state officials left any restrictions up to the discretion of individual counties. Then, on April 17, 2020, Florida prematurely reopened beaches on the same day that the state saw 1,400 additional cases of the virus, marking the biggest number of new infections since the crisis began. The move fueled debate between individuals willing to risk a return to "business as usual" quickly and those determined to follow public health safety recommendations with the notion that human lives were more important than the economy.

Florida was not the only state embroiled in political turmoil. Protestors with Democratic governors first held rallies against stay-at-home measures in Minnesota, Michigan and Virginia. President Trump responded that stringent lockdown orders were "too tough" in several U.S. states and then wrote on Twitter that people should "liberate." Additional protests swarmed across America and it was heartbreaking to see how desperate our citizens had become to return to work. Many claimed that their constitutional rights were being violated, while others used to occasion to raise concerns about the second amendment with regard to firearms. Governors across the U.S. were being pressured about how and when to reopen their states, with most opting to do so in stages or phases. However, some states and certain municipalities had to reverse their re-openings and mandate that masks be worn in public.

Florida had to suspend alcohol consumption in bars again after a massive, single-day increase of 9,000 cases in late June. It was the most for any state since the pandemic began. Then, Newsweek reported that the coronavirus had killed more people in one month in Florida and Texas than 20 years of hurricanes. Florida continued to break records for the number of positive cases and, following the 4th of July holiday, the state became the new Covid-19 epicenter. Health administration officials noted that the numbers exceeded the peak of daily cases New York reported when the pandemic exploded there in early April. On Sunday, July 12th, Florida surpassed the United States coronavirus record for the most new cases in one day. By August 11th , Florida broke another record, recording 277 deaths in just one day, and surpassing 10,000 resident deaths nearing the end of the month.

There were also growing concerns about a possible overload on health care facilities along with inadequate testing measures and medical supplies. Historically, as the number of cases continued to increase at an alarming rate all across the world, the epicenter of the disease moved from China to Europe and then America became the next target. By Easter weekend, the United States surpassed Italy with the largest number of coronavirus deaths. Congress and the White House passed emergency funding measures to help cover payrolls, unemployment and direct aid to families. However, call centers offering temporary assistance for necessities like rent and utilities were immediately overwhelmed with too many requests. It was apparent, essentially in matter of a few weeks, that far too many families were living in poverty and were literally just one paycheck away from complete disaster. The $600 a week Federal Pandemic Unemployment Compensation expired at the end of July. According to the Washington Post, this may have affected 31 million Americans during government negotiations for additional aid. Roughly 18 percent of the U.S. workforce was receiving some sort of unemployment assistance.

In addition, Covid-19 was linked to a hunger pandemic caused by economic hardship, price hikes and substantial breaks in the food chain. Many areas around the world could be facing multiple famines of biblical proportions. By the end of 2020, experts predict that upwards of 265 million people could be on the brink of starvation globally, with Africa, the Middle East and Asia being the most at risk. This will require an international response and protection of funding for major humanitarian organizations.

As of the middle of August, the U.S. recorded more than 5.5 million cases of the coronavirus, a figure that represented a quarter of the worldwide total. Sadly, America also had the most reported deaths, according to John Hopkins University. Five states accounted for more than 40% of the infections, including California, New York, Florida, Texas and Georgia. Although researchers at the University of Washington believed case counts may have peaked in the hardest-hit states, they were predicting that the number of Covid-19 related deaths in the United States could reach 300,000 by December.

The Pacific island of New Zealand was listed as one of the safest places in the world after going 102 days without community transmission. However, officials placed Auckland under lockdown following a new cluster of active infections. Vietnam went three months without detecting any new cases and then had another outbreak. Australia had to go into a six week lockdown due to a second wave of infections in Melbourne after lapses in managed isolation and quarantining facilities. Overall, European countries had the highest case-fatality ratios based on population. Age and access to care are major risk factors that influence the per capita death rate, so Covid-19 has been especially harsh in the United Kingdom, Belgium and Italy.

As the end of summer was near, educational systems around the globe faced tough decisions about how to create safe learning environments and offer quality instruction. Many public school districts in the U.S. initially gave parents a choice between online courses or returning to the classroom. Some districts split the time and the number of students attending on certain days, while others attempted a semi-regular schedule with extra precautions. Indiana, Mississippi, Tennessee and Georgia were among the first states to re-open schools and quarantines quickly followed. Local teachers unions held protests and demonstrations across the country to press for virtual learning in places where virus cases were still high. Their efforts meant that almost all of America's largest districts started the school year with an online format.

Likewise, many colleges had to reverse plans for regular operations. UNC-Chapel Hill, Notre Dame and Michigan State were among the first universities to change to remote learning after spikes in positive Covid-19 tests among students back on campus. Although rooms were held to 60% capacity and classroom seats to 30%, UNC still had a 13.6% positive test rate and 135 new cases within the first week, forcing students into quarantine dorms.

Of course, everyone involved was concerned about the social, emotional and behavioral health of our children, along with their academic achievement. Simply put, kids missed their friends and the in-person interaction. Many benefitted from special services, after-school programs and extracurricular activities. Like the coronavirus itself, low-income, minority and children living with disabilities could be disproportionately harmed because they were far more likely to rely on school-supported resources. In addition, some students do not participate in distance learning and when they disappear, educators may have limited options for locating families due to gaps in contact information.

Despite the flow of some doomsday and apocalyptic predictions, positive advice also began emerging suggesting that this "down time" might be viewed as an opportunity to bring families and communities closer together. We could go grocery shopping for an elderly neighbor, donate essential supplies to nonprofit organizations, volunteer with food banks or buy gift certificates from local businesses.

Most impressively, the crisis provided a chance to re-examine our core values and beliefs. There was a growing resurgence in the comfort of prayer, meditation and placing faith in God or a higher power. All of us certainly had the occasion to consider the people, places and things that occupied the highest priorities in our lives. Personally, I asked forgiveness for all the day-to-day blessings and special events that I had so easily taken for granted. These included things like eating out with my friends, enjoying a concert in the park, attending sporting events and celebrating at Disney with my precious great-nieces. Even going shopping for necessities or running mundane errands were privileges that I should have been thankful for doing.

Now that we had all been plunged into an alternate reality, I was especially grateful for the major obstacles in my life that had best prepared me for any challenge. Most of us face hardships that eventually define our character, influence our personality and adjust our way of thinking. This virus forced us all into new behaviors, but my spiritual awakening had already provided a solid foundation for handling changing circumstances, whether they were negative origins provoking worry or positive sources providing inspiration. This was no easy transformation, nor was it a simple journey to glance into self-discovery. Full restoration required a complete willingness to break down every aspect of my mind and body. I had to embrace the most humble existence to acknowledge every past mistake and repair relationships. I had to identify all my flaws, shortcomings and defects and then search my inner soul for the talents, assets and support systems to produce the confidence levels necessary to beat all the odds against my recovery. It was no small undertaking and the statistics certainly were not in my favor.

Those battling mental illness and substance abuse were clearly at greater risk for worsening symptoms, regression and relapse due to isolation and the uncertainty that fuels the fire of paranoia, phobias, anxiety and loneliness. Experts suggested limiting news coverage, developing new routines, exercising and focusing on pursuing different hobbies. Of course, modern technology also provided many methods to stay connected. There were on-line meetings, tele-conferences and video chats. Popular health and wellness apps began offering free services. Old fashioned phone calls were utilized again along with daily check-in methods to touch base with friends and family members. In addition, there were crisis hotlines and counselors available 24/7 through text messaging.

Although encouraging, would these measures be enough for those that completely relied upon the close personal contact within support groups, the reassuring smile from their therapist, and hugging or holding hands with those they trusted the most? Would we be able to communicate and share our deepest emotions with an open heart from a distance for an extended period of time? The answer is that the stress and feelings provoked by this crisis are already familiar to many of us. It is just that these happenings are not imagined or the result of some impairing substance or caused by a chemical imbalance in our brains. The Covid-19 threat is not a delusional hallucination or a horrifying psychotic episode.

This is the real deal and everyone is at risk on some level. We have the interpersonal tools to acknowledge and cope with the social effects. Many of us struggling with mental illness and addiction had certainly already experienced quarantine; it was just in the form of psychiatric hospitals, treatment centers and jail cells. In The Art of War, Sun Tzu wrote: "If you know the enemy and know yourself, you need not fear the results of a hundred battles." So, perhaps we are even more prepared than the "normal folks" out there for these difficult transitions and trying situations. We just have to utilize this time to revitalize previous triumphs and empower all our inner strengths again. No matter how painful our past experiences have been, it's important to revisit traumatic events and look backwards to see how far we have come through faith in our endurance. Most of us have learned that courage is not the absence of fear, it is the belief that there is always something greater than fear.

This crisis will reveal a lot about the world and our leaders, but more significantly, it will magnify our intimate levels of consciousness through our own responses. Whether it be religious faith or trust in an idea or goal, we must become deeply committed to strongly held beliefs about our own capabilities for renewal. We are all worried and unbalanced, but we can learn to value our intuition with an inner compass to help create a reliable base of support for (and from) others.

Just as children began creating rainbows to spread a cheerful windows campaign from England to Italy to New York City during the virus lockdowns, we can each discover our own unique area of encouragement in this crisis. Our personal involvement may spark enthusiasm for positive responses similar to the popular slogans kids have written to go along with their colorful rainbows. One favorite is simply: "Be confident and be brave."

Most notably, we can seek reassurance from the historic achievements of those before us who overcame insurmountable obstacles. Consider the Great Depression, the contributions of our veterans and the uplifting stories from cancer survivors as a few examples for providing inspired motivation. This is also the absolute perfect time to reflect and embrace the progress and potential demonstrated by our ancestors.

It is an occasion to remember that the freedoms, modern conveniences and lasting traditions that are now most relevant to us were passed down through generations of determined effort and generous sacrifice.

Now each of us will have a story to share to engage others as to who and what became the driving force in our lives within this pandemic. Surely, we can begin a new journey by first looking at the rugged paths carved by our own cultural history and heritage.

CHAPTER TWO

Past Triumph

Retracing the steps and accomplishments of my relatives brought a sense of calmness and peace in the wake of the current crisis. It was a humbling and joyful experience at the same time. I was the direct descendent of noble, diligent and generous people on both sides of my family. If I had inherited even a fraction of their tenacity, devotion to honest core values and determination for progress, then I could certainly learn to negotiate any storm.

This experiment of researching the past influences even produced a different prayer that every level of my existence might be shielded with the strength and dignity exhibited by my ancestors. I also came to understand that my individual response to the Covid-19 outbreak would not be nearly as important as my contribution to an overall, collective effort producing results for healing and stability in the best interests of others. There were plenty of examples within my own family tree and I now cherished them with a heart full of gratitude and a sincere desire to become a more vocal advocate for those in need.

I had the privilege to know all four of my grandparents and three of my great-grandparents. My maternal great-grandmother, Miss Polly Presnell, was born a few years after the end of the Civil War. My people were simple, hardworking farmers that wanted no part in any conflict. They did not join the confederacy, but also did not wish to branded traitors by the federal government. They knew very little, if anything, about slavery and they certainly had no close proximity to any wealthy plantation owners. They survived in the extremely rural and isolated area of the Appalachian Mountains of western North Carolina. This location has the highest altitude east of the Mississippi River, along with rocky terrain and exceptionally harsh winters.

Although secluded enough to avoid most national disruptions, remnants of the war reached the area in the summer of 1863. At that time, east Tennessee was abandoned by confederate soldiers and some Unionist along with dissidents (those who chose to support neither the North nor the South) banded together to attack the community. My great-grandmother passed down the story from her parents about how the desperate gang randomly fired bullets across the landscape and entered homes to steal valuable necessities, mostly food items, from already impoverished families. The worst part of the scenario was they were intent on leaving innocent people with absolutely nothing to eat, so these rogue thieves ruined what they did not want or could not immediately utilize. Specifically, they poured out all the flour and sugar onto floors and urinated on everything to render the limited provisions completely useless. This incident must have left an indelible impression because I remember hearing the story as a child from my grandmother.

Perhaps it helped spark some broad stroke of independence in my great-grandmother because she was a true pioneer with great resilience. Miss Polly was of Native American heritage with a dominant Cherokee Indian bloodline. Most notably, she was a devoted single parent against all the odds during a time period when being alone was unheard of and virtually impossible financially. By the early 1900's, she was raising seven children all by herself. She provided for her family by living off the land and that required a lot of rigorous manual labor to include pulling and drying witch hazel and bead wood leaves that could be boiled down into oils. She also harvested Galax, an evergreen perennial plant, which was used to treat cuts and kidney ailments. These items would be sold to the "medicine man" (Native American shamanistic healer). My great-grandmother also had to be industrious and ingenious with other projects to get by, so she hand-knotted and braided rag rugs from wool, cotton and old fabric strips. Her creations became so popular that she was able to market them to wealthy northerners and also traded them to get nice clothing for the children.

She became a successful entrepreneur, skilled business-woman and keen negotiator and she did so without ever having a husband. Of course, since she did refuse several marriage proposals, she was the topic of some wide-spread speculation. It was even rumored that she had murdered one of her alleged boyfriends and disposed of his body because he had abruptly disappeared from the area. He had simply abandoned the family, but the accusation persisted for years. Decades later, a U.S. census bureau report finally revealed that he was alive and well, living with a wife and other children, in the state of Virginia.

Regardless of all the hardships, my great-grandmother saved money and bargained enough to buy 13 acres of land with an amazing scenic view not too far from the Watauga River. She constructed a modest home and this area would eventually be deemed within the state's final county of Avery in

1911. One could even argue that she was blessed to rediscover some of the property taken from her own ancestors, since the mountain region of western North Carolina was the center of the Cherokee homeland before the arrival of Europeans.

My maternal grandparents, known as Ma and Pa Ward, also built their home on the property. Together, they grew most of their own food, planted apple trees, picked berries, raised tobacco and kept livestock. When my great-grandmother Polly became ill in 1935, she was ready with a final act that further demonstrated her strength in the face of pain and grief. In order to prepare for her own death, she traded one of her prize possessions, an engraved pistol with a pearl handle, to a local woodworker in exchange for constructing her coffin. She made her own funeral arrangements as soon as she was diagnosed with cancer. She was able to hold one grandson briefly prior to her death. My grandmother's first child, Marion, passed away a few hours after he was born. She lost another son, Tommy, who was stillborn many years later.

My grandparents survived through the Great Depression mostly through living off of the abundant resources of the land. They were accustomed to the challenges of poverty, as the lumber industry faded soon after World War I and other regional employers, like businesses operating with coal and textiles, struggled with overproduction, low wages and rising unemployment throughout the 1920's. Finally, Franklin D. Roosevelt brought progress to the area under his New Deal with WPA projects. In the late 1930's, my family worked on the large stone building that would become Beech Mountain Elementary School, and it was constructed on a hill that basically adjoined my grandparent's property. Forty some years later, my sister and I would receive the majority of our secondary education at that very facility.

My grandfather primarily made a living hauling coal and lime. In his travels, he also attended auctions and bought and sold everything from antiques to car parts to farm equipment. Pa Ward had a jovial and outgoing personality with a penchant for telling long and humorous stories. Most of his business associates were also his friends and he had a reputation for being honest and fair with all his bargaining transactions. During the time of World War II, my grandfather was relieved from serving because he was the primary breadwinner for such a large family. Two of my great-uncles did join the effort overseas and my grandfather was blessed to have both his brothers return home unharmed.

My grandmother worked tirelessly in a huge garden, canned fruits and vegetables and prepared food around the clock. She was well known as one of the best cooks anywhere, so people had a habit of visiting around noontime because they knew she would invite them to eat. She was also a mysterious self-made southern chef because she never looked at a recipe and never wrote down any of the ingredients.

Ma Ward only had a 3rd grade education and never learned to drive, but she knew every single passage throughout the entire Bible and studied it on a daily basis. Reading from God's word was one of her cherished routines. Sunday was the only day that she did not do laundry or regular housework because it was the Sabbath, but she did prepare huge family meals for relatives and guests nearly every weekend.

She was also known for her generosity in collecting items that others might need. She actually had a small shed that everyone lovingly referred to as "the junk house." It was stocked full with a variety of clothing, shoes, household items and knick-knacks. The footwear was of particular importance because my grandmother always said wearing the wrong shoes could ruin an entire outfit and even make your hair look bad. Community members loved shopping in that little barn full of hidden treasurers. They could load an entire grocery bag full of items for a nickel or maybe a dime. Of course, those who could not spare a few cents could choose what they wanted or needed for free.

Some of Ma Ward's favorite customers were those most ostracized, forgotten or ridiculed in the community. For example, one gentleman that frequently visited my grandmother had a speech impediment and was less advanced in his mental and social development. He had a gentle, kind and simple nature, especially because my grandma went out of her way to initiate a good conversation and always encourage him to smile more often. Unfortunately, many in the area referred to him only as a "retarded queer" because he sometimes chose to wear feminine attire. Grandma never judged him and, in fact, she would always set aside the nicest, most ornate, embroidered or extravagant dresses she could find and reserve them just for him.

My grandma was seldom likely to notice faults or point out peculiarities in others. She did possess a sixth sense about the character and integrity of area residents, however. She had an uncanny ability to know about any indiscretions or infidelities in the neighborhood and this knowledge did not come from idle chatter because she did not participate in gossip. Her insights usually turned out to be accurate, especially with regard to hidden agendas or secret romances. Some thought she might have psychic abilities. Most likely, Ma Ward was keenly observant, adept at sensing even the smallest of white lies, and overly empathetic to the feelings and emotions of others. Whatever her special gift was, my mother must have inherited it because my sister and I could rarely, if ever, fool her. Even our most clever and detailed stories designed to cover rebellious, adolescent behaviors were quickly exposed by Mom.

My mother ended up being the youngest of six children, with only one brother and four sisters. The better part of her childhood, she was raised without electricity or indoor plumbing. The family finally had a television in 1955, but there was only one channel and that was NBC broadcasting from Bristol, Tennessee. There was not a telephone in the home until 1963, which was the year my Mom completed high school. It was a party line that had to be shared with several other neighbors and was installed so late because utility companies did not offer service in the remote area.

Although Mom had few extravagances growing up, she was close to her siblings, developed an amazing work ethic and was determined with a positive attitude about her future. She devoted herself to self-improvement and diligent schoolwork. When her high school boyfriend was deployed to Vietnam, she maintained her composure and was steadfast in establishing her independence. Mom was a straight A student and finished third in her class. The night of her graduation, my grandfather suggested that she should consider going to college. By that time, Mom had other plans and more creative visions, especially with regard to financial security. She had known limited resources and did not want to end up employed in a factory or barely surviving on a farm somewhere.

Mom was grateful for the strong core values, religious faith and the importance of genuine loyalty that she had learned through her experiences. She would come to especially treasure the shielded environment of her youth upon moving to the nation's capital. However, Washington, D.C. was the heartbeat of progress, restlessness, civil discord and new opportunities all at the same time in the 1960's. Mom was moving to this exciting, thriving and exhilarant place during one of the most prolific decades in American history. She may have been arriving as a "country bumpkin", but she was sharp, determined and confident. She also was not totally embarking into this territory completely alone because two of her older sisters were already living there. Most importantly, Mom's relocation set her directly on a path of destiny where she would meet my Dad.

My paternal grandparents, known as Grandma and Pa Marshall, were raised in central Pennsylvania and dedicated the majority of their entire lives to community and civic service. My Dad was the middle child, with two older brothers and two younger sisters. One of his earliest memories is of railroad employees, homeless individuals and migrant workers lining up on the back porch of the home where my grandparents always fed them during the years surrounding the Great Depression.

Professionally, Pa Marshall owned a car dealership and a scrap metal business. Grandma began her career in broadcasting, hosting her own children's educational television show, where she organized youth talent shows to entertain area organizations, clubs, nursing homes and hospitals. She was the narrator for the South York County Male Chorus and an active member of the Matinee Musical Club.

For nearly three decades, my grandma also ran the York County Rescue Mission serving the homeless, hungry and financially challenged through recovery, renewal, restoration and re-engagement. She partnered with local churches and other nonprofits for donations to operate a huge thrift store, offer crisis intervention, and assist in locating affordable housing. The mission operated as a Christian outreach initiative, so grandma also taught Bible study classes and developed a reading program for the visually impaired. Her devotion to the disadvantaged extended to her personal arena of faith where she convinced religious leaders that those with developmental disabilities, mental illness and other health challenges could benefit from a special fellowship within a church environment. My grandpa Marshall procured a large bus and consistently rounded all the neighborhoods early every Sunday morning to pick up participants. My grandma was the group facilitator and Sunday school teacher for a gathering that continued to grow and flourish throughout the years.

Grandma's commitment to community service and political involvement spanned a vast range of interests, including some that were controversial. Long before Mothers Against Drunk Driving, my grandmother helped develop a regional temperance movement that included vocal opposition against new liquor stores and organized efforts to prevent local restaurants from getting permits to sell alcohol. She was a member of the Women's Christian Temperance Union and lobbied for laws against the availability of alcohol during certain days and hours, along with taking a stance of complete prohibition wherever possible. The group created promise to abstinence agreements and asked parents, especially young mothers, to sign statements vowing to teach their children about the dangers of drinking while also taking an oath that no alcohol would be allowed in the family environment. My mom declined participation because she could not predict what my sister and I might be exposed to in the future, nor could she swear under an oath to God that we would never touch a drop of alcohol in our lifetimes.

Grandma Marshall believed that alcohol was the underlying cause of all types of social problems to include poverty, domestic violence and unemployment. It was also a deeply personal cause because her father and three brothers were desperate, life-long alcoholics. She grew up watching how alcohol ruined jobs, relationships and opportunities. However, my grandma was a champion in her faith for renewal at any age and under any circumstances. She dedicated her life works to the premise that positive change was attainable regardless of the obstacles and she demonstrated this mindset through her own priorities in leadership.

At the age of 75, grandma decided to continue her education because she had never received a high school diploma. She took classes in core subjects while also studying information processing, problem solving and critical thinking skills. She had certainly already proven that she was adept in these areas, but this was still an enormous undertaking that required a lot of determination. She easily passed the battery of tests and was awarded her GED. In October of 1991, she received a personal letter of congratulations from President George H.W. Bush where he commended her for the dedication and hard work she had devoted, while also labeling her a wonderful example and stating that we should all be students for life.

She then went on to become the first woman to be elected to the Dallastown Council. She served as council chaplain and was instrumental in the development of land for recreational parks.

Grandma Marshall contributed her time and energies to so many organizations and programs for the disadvantaged that the House of Representative for the Commonwealth of Pennsylvania, along with the Governor's office, presented her with a special recognition for her achievements on her 80th birthday in 1996. She was honored for her service to the Navy Mothers of America, VA hospitals, the American Red Cross, the Mental Health Association, the Indian Steps Museum, the memorial library, the local PTA, and the Girl

Scouts. In her spare time, she had also managed to become a published poet and was rather famous for writing letters to legislators about a myriad of topics.

It had truly never occurred to me how much my maternal and paternal grandparents had in common, especially my grandmothers. They had a normal inclination to reach out to those most disenfranchised. They were committed to making their communities more progressive through helping others. They consistently demonstrated care and decency through productive deeds, words and actions. Here my relatives were certainly divided by culture, geography, socio-economic status and circumstances, yet they were so similar in their faith for generous responses to those most in need and togetherness for the best interest of all during any challenges. They were able to blend the concepts of grass-roots organizing, education and cultural assimilation to create better outcomes.

My grandparents endured the Great Depression and they exemplified what President Franklin D. Roosevelt declared when he said: "True patriotism urges us to build an even more substantial America where the good things of life are shared by more of us and where social injustices will not be encouraged to flourish." It was the type of response desperately required within the core response to Covid-19 because we were now the generation that had a rendezvous with destiny. Would we arise from this devastating seclusion with a renewed compassion to rebuild a better environment for everyone?

FDR led the United States through the Great Depression and World War II with an international vision based on shared experiences for overcoming hardships through our common aspirations. He stated, "Since the beginning of American history, we have engaged in change, in a perpetual revolution, a revolution which goes on steadily, quietly adjusting itself to changing conditions without the concentration camp or the quicklime in the ditch. The world order which we seek is the cooperation of free countries, working together in a friendly, civilized society." How comforting those words would have been in the midst of the coronavirus outbreak. In the time of FDR, Americans did not fail their country nor their neighbors nor themselves. Now the question becomes do we have the unity of purpose to defeat this invisible disease and deal appropriately with the economic aftermath? Would Americans go "all out" to provide the necessities and materials required for victory over Covid-19 and protect the most vulnerable? Most importantly, would we come together as a nation to permanently improve the lifestyles of everyone with a focus on those most disadvantaged? Would we make compromises in the best interests of others, admit our shortcomings, and suffer our disappointments and losses together, while remembering our nation's historic purpose and promises?

Initially, we were already embroiled in political turmoil within an environment that seemed increasingly void of any moderate ideology. We had become angrily divided and labeled as right-winged conservatives or left-winged liberals with no middle ground for negotiations. The reactionaries tried to further convolute the responses to Covid-19 from every angle. Health policy advisors were ignored. Medical experts were questioned. Economic forecasts were scrutinized. Social media was flooded with ridiculous accusations, misleading information, dangerous predictions, outlandish conspiracy theories and malicious stories leading to increased fears and frustrations. Yet within this international crisis, there was still a looming hope of opportunity to once again compel each other to progressively enhance the American democratic way of life.

The coronavirus demonstrated, in a matter of a few weeks, that living wages, guaranteed health care for all, enhanced unemployment benefits, increased social security benefits and fair labor rights were not revolutionary, partisan issues, but rather just plain common sense. Covid-19 forced record numbers of millions of Americans to file for unemployment and half of those individuals may have lost their employer-sponsored health insurance due to layoffs. Opening a special enrollment period for federal Affordable Care Act marketplace exchanges was a plan that did not materialize, and it would seem that looking back in history would prove useful as to why we would have to pull together a collective response for renewal at all levels of government.

In 1935, there were those that believed social security was an unnecessary, radical concept. Even many Americans didn't fully trust or understand the plan for a public pension program. Some politicians labeled it a fraudulent tax bill, while others insisted it would never be saved and was just a cruel hoax on the workforce forcing the country closer to socialism. Three decades later, when the Social Security Act amendments were signed by President Johnson in 1965 creating Medicare and Medicaid, the same opposition was voiced declaring that it was socialized medicine.

In the past decade, Obamacare has not fixed most of the problems with America's market-based healthcare system but Medicaid expansion has saved lives and so has the ban on discriminating against people with pre-existing conditions. Sadly, the Trump administration is eliminating the shields for gay and transgender individuals, removing protections for sex and gender identity. This means that LGBTQ patients might not be able to access the care they need, putting the health and wellbeing of vulnerable people at risk.

In this pandemic, perhaps it would be helpful to determine exactly how we define socialism, since there are differences in regulating, mandating, assisting and totally controlling. It might be possible that we would all just agree that there are various types of government intervention and that some of them are absolutely necessary in the best interests of the people.

The Coronavirus Aid, Relief and Economic Security (CARES) Act was intended to be a temporary stimulus, stop-gap measure, but it is the largest program in American history to aid citizens and companies. Legislators also passed another 484 billion dollar relief package to assist small businesses and hospitals. However, some are concerned that huge corporate bailouts may not benefit the average American. This is a valid consideration given the mistakes in the 2008 rescue and recovery efforts where profits bounced back quickly for the largest conglomerates and most working people did not see their conditions improve.

Covid-19 has exposed the extreme injustices and inequalities of our economic and social system, so we should be going beyond attempting to restore the pre-crisis status quo and be outspoken about what the new conditions of returning to "normal" will look like. After all, a lot of the reason for the emergency intervention was the delayed response from federal and state governments in dealing with this crisis. Surely, there is now uniform consensus that we were not prepared and this led to unprecedented cultural, financial and psychological shock. In the future, we must invest in better health care systems with pandemic response units to swiftly identify and contain outbreaks. We must have production of medical equipment and supplies along with enhanced, ongoing pharmaceutical research. We need the capabilities to perform large-scale testing and monitoring of diseases in connection with improving lab processing operations.

From an interpersonal perspective, we must also have the necessary plans and support systems in place to reintegrate into workplaces, schools, businesses, our social interactions and our daily routines. The coronavirus has, and will continue to have, a profound effect on our mental health and how we interact with others. We have all been subjected to isolation, loneliness, anxiety and stress for an extended period of time. Psychiatric experts have long warned that these conditions, along with depression, lead to increased substance abuse, suicidal thoughts, self-harm and other consequences, such as homelessness. Alcohol sales in the U.S. have increased by 55%, and crisis lines and nonprofit organizations have been overwhelmed with desperate callers. We have been living in trauma and it is abundantly clear that we need additional mental health providers, therapists, counselors, social workers and trained volunteers. Individuals working in these occupations should be more appreciated and better compensated for transforming families and saving lives. We also require a system in place for "moment-to-moment" or "real-time" monitoring for those already struggling so that coping tools can be accessed quickly to help people at home.

Our heath care workers, who have continually sacrificed and exhausted all their best efforts for us, certainly deserve to have special protections and resources to address post-traumatic stress, along with other incentives that sincerely address the occupational hazards that they are expected to endure. Likewise, we owe an eternal debt of gratitude to those workers deemed essential, while extended our greatest reform efforts to those labeled non-essential and losing their source of income. Both categories represent our fellow Americans who are underpaid, underinsured and taken for granted. The argument for raising the minimum wage has never been more evident. Employers should respond with merit-based systems, extra bonuses, extended paid leave policies, educational opportunities and greater advancement initiatives with additional supplements and perks to benefits packages.

In this period of great tribulation, most of us have taken some time to examine where we are as individuals and what we want for the future. Aside from the painful separations from our family, friends, co-workers, neighbors and colleagues, we were ultimately alone (at least in our reflections and thoughts) and forced to consider the best and worst possible outcomes about how our lives would change. We were all just propelled into a journey of self-discovery, whether we wanted to explore ourselves or not. We may react differently at various times, but certainly each of us wanted relief from the constant pressures and inconvenient adjustments. With no warning, some of us had to work from home, negotiate school assignments for our children and rearrange every aspect of our entire lives.

Still, somewhere and sometime during this ongoing crisis, our sense of priorities may have been shifting or even questioned. Of course, we were frustrated, bored and confused. Some of us even felt like prisoners in our own homes and the growing political and civil unrest contributed to additional worry about the state of our nation. It appeared that we might be unraveling as a country instead of uniting against this hideous disease. Some even believed that the coronavirus itself was not the real enemy and that opened the door to blaming a vast array of other people, places and things for the crisis. We all sought comfort and release from fear, yet we could not even agree about how to define the real threats, let alone create a common ground for solutions. However, in those quieter, most serene of honest moments, did we ponder another universe, consider a different course of action, or wonder about things we have never been willing to discuss before?

It is possible that we might have the perfect occasion to focus on our positive attributes, celebrate our past achievements and develop a new mindset of hope for optimistic outcomes. It is also possible that we might even become the best versions of ourselves through these difficult transitions. Our ancestors certainly contributed to the greater good, and we will see and share the stories of many heroic efforts emerging from the Covid-19 crisis.

We can learn to listen without judgement, speak without prejudice, help without expectations, understand without pretension and love without conditions. Is there an initiative to assist us within the full realm of self-discovery where we can also offer our finest personal gifts to improving the lives of others? The answer is yes. There is a program model for that. It is not sponsored by the government, connected with any religious denomination, involved in politics or allied with any organization or institution. It is an outline that prepares us for any crisis and fulfills the promises for the greatest life possible.

CHAPTER THREE

Raising Voices

My Dad joined the Navy straight out of high school. He studied aviation mechanics and served his tour of duty aboard the USS Hornet during the Eisenhower Administration. Upon his discharge, he secured a position with United Airlines in the nation's capital. His love of cars and fascination with Harley Davidson motorcycles prompted him to also work part-time for a service station. As fate would have it, Mom frequently went to that particular service station because it was close to her day time job. She was employed by an accounting firm, and was also an evening clerk at Hecht's Department Store.

It did not take Dad long to boldly suggest that maybe Mom should take him out to lunch in return for the detailed attention he had been devoting to her car. Mom was initially taken aback by such a brazen statement. It briefly occurred to her that he might be one of those big city perverts that she had been warned about. He was certainly outside her experienced culture because no Southern gentleman would dream of suggesting that a woman should pay for a meal at a restaurant. He also had tattoos, which could have been an indication of serving prison time. Despite these reservations, there was something about this man that Mom inherently trusted. He had kind eyes and mannerisms that seemed genuine and humorous at the same time. Mom liked Dad's upbeat personality and found his smile to be somewhat captivating. She eventually consented to going with him to Top's Diner. After all, it was an open, busy, public place that was safely located right down the street. Their relationship rapidly flourished into a union that could only be outlined in the most descriptive of romance novels. Of course, Dad did initially have to eliminate some competition for Mom's affection. On one occasion, he forcefully escorted a "would be" suitor with a bouquet of flowers straight back to the curb, as the saying goes. This poor fella arrived at Mom's apartment unannounced while my Dad happened to be there.

My parents had a brief engagement and exchanged vows quietly before a preacher on Memorial Day of 1966. They decided on an apartment in Oxon Hill, Maryland and then I was born (a blessed accident) in May of 1967. In those days, no one was allowed in the delivery room, so my Dad and my maternal Aunt Margie nervously chain smoked awaiting my arrival 20 some hours later. I weighed eight pounds and nine ounces. Mom said her labor pains were so horrific that she actually tried to run away from the hospital. To this day, I do not have a clear answer as to why they chose to call me April. I suspect it came from a nurses' name badge while Mom was a bit delirious, but they both deny this and insist there was some serious consideration given in the process of picking out a name. So, I really never liked the month of April because I always heard my name and thought someone was talking to me. April Fool's Day was a real blast for me every year too.

I was also born with two, port-wine stain birthmarks on the right side of my face. The dominant one is located just below my eye and the smaller mark is right beside my nose. It is kind of like having permanent pieces of a map outline or jigsaw puzzle to wear around all the time. I am very accustomed to them now and fancy that they are somehow special and make me more unique, maybe like having a tattoo from God. However, I have spent my entire life explaining my appearance to others and answering questions like, "Did you win the fight?", "Who hit you?", "Oh my God, what happened to your face?", "Did you fall?", "What kind of accident were you in?", "Where did you get the shiner?", and "What did you do to yourself girl?" My favorite one is, "You should get away from the person that did that to your face!" I actually like that reaction because at least it shows some level of awareness about domestic violence.

As a toddler, I received a lot of attention and I was not especially overjoyed when my sister came along almost three years later. By that time, Mom and Dad had their own house, but I still cherish the time spent living with my grandparents and the close interactions with aunts, uncles and cousins.

I was extremely jealous of this new baby in the home and Mom had to watch me all the time so that I would not pinch or bite my sister. I even reverted in my toilet training and had to go back to diapers for a short period of time. Once I actually slapped Mom in the face when she was resting on the couch. Mom popped me right back and she said I just sat on the floor, staring at her intently. It was odd that I did not cry, show any emotion or say anything. I didn't answer any of her questions and just continued glaring at her. Perhaps this was an early warning sign of some sort, but maybe just sparked the beginning of sibling rivalry.

My sister and I were enrolled in the private Christian school at the same church where Grandma Marshall taught her class for those with mental and physical challenges.

The school was a rigid and frightening setting. By first grade, I was an overweight, insecure and shy child. Part of my timid nature was the direct result of the overly strict environment and the intimidating, zealous pastor in charge. He was a fire and brimstone preacher who predicted a certain eternal damnation for the majority of the population. His fixation on the devil and a burning hell full of torture was terrifying to me. Although I was happy to be baptized at six years of age, I still was not sure I was going to make it to heaven. I had nightmares about demons and was horrified of dying because Satan might be waiting to take me down beneath the earth to that dark and painful place. Nearly every sermon, the pastor said that people who thought they were saved really were not. Even the Methodists and Catholics were leading folks straight to hell, according to his regular rantings. He would yell and scream while perspiring, turning red in the face and banging his fists on the pulpit. These outbursts had no impact on my grandparents whatsoever. In fact, Grandma Marshall said she was so grateful for her hearing aids because she would just turn them all the way down whenever the preacher started one of his rampages. My Grandpa Marshall typically slept through the service. Mom and Dad were patiently tolerant, as they thought, deep down, that he was sincere about leading others to Jesus, even if his methods were extreme. However, just because our pastor had knowledge of Biblical scriptures did not necessarily make him the ideal candidate for an education administrator, especially since he did not seem to grasp the concept of age-appropriate materials.

Logically, most of the teachers and staff at the school were also harsh and adhered to an authoritarian structure to instill fear, discipline and full control. Corporal punishment was a constant threat and I had no idea if any of my classmates were as distressed as I was because friendships were not allowed either. We were to just continually line up and follow orders without ever talking to one another. Once I misplaced a little pocketbook and would not admit it was mine because I knew there would be repercussions. Losing or leaving anything was a huge offense. I waited for months until the church finally announced their lost and found items and asked my Dad to take me so I could get it back. Even then, a staff member chastised me for failing to take responsibility sooner. Dad ignored her comments and just held my hand to leave the building.

Finally, I garnered the courage to tell Mom that I was drastically afraid and when I shared the abusive details, *the real hell* actually broke loose. My mother informed everyone at that school that there would be no more nap times in a completely dark room with the door locked. She made them take down all the thick construction paper that blocked any light from coming through the windows and doors with glass panes. Furthermore, I would be allowed to go to the restroom anytime I wanted with or without their permission. They would immediately stop playing the story of Bambi on the record player over and over again because it was upsetting to children and, frankly, redundant. Finally, I was to never be punished or threatened for any lost notes pinned to my dress. In fact, there would be no more such correspondence on my person and if the school wanted to contact her, they could pick up the telephone or use the United States Post Office.

That summer, Mom cut off all our hair and dressed us in matching short sets complete with tank tops. My sister and I looked totally out of place on Sundays and the pastor went out of his way to call us little boys. Mom reminded him that it was indeed hot outside and the confines of the school dress code could not be enforced during the summer. I swear Mom did it as an act of defiance against the entire church/school establishment, but she still maintains it was a simple matter of the weather.

These earliest years helped to form a persisting distinction between organized religion, different faiths and even patterns of behavior. I learned, and still believe, that Christians should be "Christ-like" and that would be synonymous with compassion for others, exhibiting mercy, forgiveness and abounding in love. Within the current times, it seems the entire term of Christianity has taken on a whole new definition. Many have even stopped calling themselves Christians because, although they are followers of Jesus, they do not wish to be aligned with the evangelical extremists or the far right conservatives. Some of these groups promote bigotry, racism, and sexism as justifiable. Some have an absolute lack of tolerance for diversity and place judgmental labels through a wide spectrum, leading to a resurgence of Xenophobia across America.

Somehow the lines between church and state have become all blurry again, and any notions of bi-partisan consent regarding political, social or ethical solutions has completely vanished. The divisions have become so stark that every Democrat must be agnostic and every Republican must be a zealot. The conservative Democrat and the liberal Republican have become extinct. We now have a binary party system that has divided the country into two irreconcilable teams and we have no way to come together on an issue-by-issue basis. Some have suggested that the only way out is to change the U.S. electoral system to allow for more parties and hope the pieces can rearrange themselves into a functional governing system. There is very little room for probabilities, we have literally become a two-party system that is to separate, design and decide our viewpoints about everything. That is frightening, right along with the new stereotypical view of being a Christian.

Now, white nationalism and white supremacy along with an array of overly armed rebel groups claim to be carrying the causes of Jesus, yet their propaganda and actions are inspiring violence and contempt for others. In fact, the number of hate groups in America has risen to a record high, growing 55% in the Trump era, according to the Southern Poverty Law Center. Hate groups are defined as organizations with beliefs and practices that demonize a class of people. This was attributed to anti-immigration rhetoric and fear mongering. Somehow these groups have become empowered through their rage and paranoia and must feel like they have been given the green light to go ahead and act on their worst instincts. The Anti-Defamation League reports that the number of rallies and demonstrations by white supremacy groups also rose dramatically between 2017 and 2018. Even the majority of mass shootings in the United States over the past couple of years have a link to right-wing extremism, according to the league. A study by the Center for Strategic and International Studies found the number of terrorist attacks quadrupled in the United States between 2016 and 2017 and that far-right attacks rose 43% in Europe over the same period.

One could easily make the argument that the very foundation of our American democracy had shifted so much that, of course, the response to Covid-19 would just keep reinforcing the same divisive politics. We should not be surprised by protestors demanding that their states reopen or those claiming that their liberties and freedoms had been violated. (Although many holding up signs like "my body, my choice" may not have realized that these are pro-choice and women's rights slogans). Some were quoted as saying, "there are more important things than living." One Texas politician said that "lots of grandparents would rather die than see the US economy suffer." Other people thought that senior citizens should "take a chance on survival for the good of others."

It may have been easy to point out the hypocrisies, but where is the voice of reason during all this turmoil? Most Americans are deeply concerned about the plight of our service workers, small businesses and all others who dramatically lost their source of income. Most also hold public safety in the highest regard, so it was certainly possible, if not probable, that the majority of us are sympathetic to all the issues surrounding Covid-19. Yet, there are very little efforts to offer negotiations, present information to enhance understanding or join together in some sort of cohesive unity. This is due to the fact that partisanship was already deeply rooted in anger and past resentment, so the coronavirus brought those frustrations to a roaring boiling point.

The challenge for progressive, rational compromise is far greater than any of us might imagine. Many of our citizens feel that their views are not being represented by either party, as evidenced by the growing number of those identifying themselves as independents. Most states still keep independent voters out of primary elections and this is another form of discrimination where both parties have abused their power as private organizations or clubs to elect representatives through a tax-funded process. The primaries are an important component of a public election process and result in leaders, who, once elected, do not just impact party members, but affect everyone. According to the Pew Research Center, Independent voters will be pivotal in the 2020 presidential election.

In fact, this year's election process has already been unprecedented with 15 states having to postpone primaries due to the pandemic. Now, we all must cast our ballots because our existence and quality of life literally depend upon it. Voter participation should be at an overall high, even though we are bravely marching forward with unsurmountable losses.

However, the U.S. Postal Service warned states that there could be potential delays delivering absentee and mail-in ballots. Some areas expected 10 times the typical volume of election mail due to the coronavirus pandemic.

The controversy raged on because the Trump administration made massive changes to the Postal Service, including a new Postmaster General that clamped down on overtime, halted late delivery trips, removed mail sorting machines and even took letter collection boxes off the streets. President Trump also blocked funding for the Postal Service and opposed mail-in ballots, alleging it could lead to voter fraud. Some states looked for ways to build more time into their systems, while others, including Pennsylvania and Michigan, called for extensions on counting late-arriving ballots in the November election.

Following bipartisan criticism regarding the disrupted operations of the United States Postal Service, congressional leaders requested an investigation by the USPS Inspector General to review policy changes, compliance with federal ethics rules and potential conflicts of interest. Lawmakers from both parties and postal union leaders began voicing concerns over the summer about slower and less reliable mail delivery (including complaints from veterans and the elderly about their medications). There were claims that the Postmaster General was intentionally undermining the capabilities of the Postal Service to sabotage mail-in voting for the election.

Many analysts have indicated that the election could drag out for an extended period of time as mail-in ballots are counted, results are contested or the apparent losing candidate refuses to concede. The unprecedented challenges of pandemic-era voting coupled with the harshly divided political landscape will test the limits of democracy and could plunge the country into a constitutional crisis. Experts suggest that Americans should prepare for disorder, confusion, protests and an array of legal battles. Law scholar and author Rick Hanson says there is no question that things are going to go wrong, as he predicts in his book, "Election Meltdown."

In the midst of struggles, we have heard very little about making Covid-19 advance care plans. Every nursing home and assisted living center should be helping residents with making decisions about the desirability for hospitalization and ventilator support. Likewise, every one of us at high risk due to age or illness should have plans about how we would like to be treated.

More Americans have now died from the coronavirus than in the Vietnam War, and it is now one of the leading causes of death in the country. Covid-19 victims have to suffer and die alone. Family and friends cannot be there and are forced to grieve silently in isolation. Sometimes, priests have the chance to administer last rights over the telephone while families are left alone at home. There are no final goodbyes, memorial services or funerals. Our healthcare professionals have to watch helplessly while they try to support a peaceful course of death for their patients suffocating from respiratory failure. Nurses are unable to even offer a gentle touch of comfort to those gasping for air as their lungs fill with fluid in acute respiratory distress. These courageous doctors and nurses will return from the frontlines, just as many of our veterans have, with post-traumatic stress disorder and a myriad of other emotional challenges. One New York emergency doctor who was treating Covid-19 patients survived the virus herself and then took her own life. She was only 49-years-old. The unimaginable stress caused by the outbreak most definitely contributed to her death.

We have to ensure that Covid-19 victims do not disappear from our memories. Their lives were not disposable nor should they be identified as numbers in a daily fatality statistic. Somehow in the chaos, we may have failed to recognize that these were real people with names and futures. These were real people with hopes, dreams and contributions. These were real people that were loved and these were real people who are desperately missed. Could we take a moment every day, even in the middle of our own personal burdens, to offer a prayer, meditation or moment of silence to reflect on their lives? It seems a small gesture to show respect and re-center our thoughts on others. This does not diminish our interpersonal struggles, but rather opens the door of possibilities to recognizing a sharing of our strengths. We can extend a conscious level of peace through searching our hearts and minds for spiritual blessings. It is possible to utilize our own gratitude list to translate encouragement to those less fortunate.

The emergence of on-line support groups and other forums to express positive reinforcements are also reassuring developments that will hopefully continue to grow in participation. For example, Facebook has a public group called the kindness pandemic with nearly 600,000 members from around the world who post uplifting stories, heroic acts and creative ways to reach out to those in need.

This crisis has pushed us all onto a new road of experiences, but we can add lights along this pathway through developing greater understanding about the elements of sorrow and the absolute power of untapped resiliency. This can represent a period of self-discovery that we might be afforded just this once in our lifetime. Maybe we should take a deep look into ourselves, our priorities and the true sources of our motivation. Perhaps we can focus on the people that mean the most to us and question the things that hinder our relationships. We can sort of interview ourselves emotionally, knowing that it is not enough to simply answer where we might like to see ourselves five years from now. The key is to venture beyond the obvious, surface reactions that we have in common with fear, apprehension and frustration. We have to be willing to expose difficult considerations such as investigating our prejudices, our judgements and our resentments.

We can begin by asking what this crisis has revealed about our personality and then move on to more reflection. What are the inherent things about my character that I would like to improve and why? Who or what influences me the most and how? How can I deal or cope with circumstances that are beyond my control? What do I want to change to become the very best version of myself? These are just preliminary thoughts so that we can start a few steps that will become an interpersonal dance with our own destiny. We must also examine our support systems and where we place our trust. Invariably, we also question our responses and reactions. These are critical components, after all, that dictate how we operate and function on a daily basis. Eventually, we get to the point of evaluating those in leadership roles. Can we lean on those in charge during this pandemic, or any other massive challenge, with full confidence that their decisions and choices are sincerely in our best interests?

Personally, I felt disconnected, confused and, at times, completely bewildered. There did not appear to be a clear, rational or comforting voice in this catastrophic storm. The only exception was a rare address given by Queen Elizabeth II that demonstrated humility and genuine compassion for people across the world. She began her speech by acknowledging the grief, financial difficulties and enormous changes. She then went on to thank frontline and healthcare workers, while also showing appreciation to those staying at home for "helping to protect the vulnerable, and sparing many families the pain already felt by those who have lost loved ones."

The Queen offered an uplifting message of victory and hope for the future by saying: "I want to reassure you that if we remain united and resolute, then we will overcome it. I hope in the years to come everyone will be able to take pride in how they responded to this challenge, and those who come after us will say the Britons of this generation were as strong as any, that the attributes of self-discipline, of quiet, good –humored resolve, and of fellow feeling still characterize this country. The pride in who we are is not a part of our past, it defines our present and our future. The moments when the United Kingdom has come together to applaud its care and essential workers will be remembered as an expression of our national spirit, and its symbol will be the rainbows drawn by children."

This is an example of the heartwarming words that exhibit generous leadership and represent the type of kind guidance that joins people together for a common endeavor. It is the type of governance that understands shared hardships, inspires successes and frames gratitude as a core value for endurance.

In early May, former President George W. Bush issued a statement calling for the end of the pandemic partisanship and asking Americans to remember the challenges of September 11, 2001. In a video message, President Bush said, "Following 9/11, I saw a great nation rise as one to honor the brave, to grieve with the grieving and to embrace unavoidable new duties. And I have no doubt, none at all, that this spirit of service and sacrifice is alive and well in America." The problem with this comparison is that we knew and could label the exact terrorists in the 9/11 attacks. Now, people were not in agreement about who or what was the real threat, so by Memorial Day weekend, the beaches and the bars were packed across the country. There was little, if any, social distancing and only employees of establishments were wearing masks.

It seemed impossible that the level of discord and disruption could get worse, but it did following horrendous tragedies that demanded, and deserved, a public outrage against racism and police brutality. The first incident involved the shooting death of 25-year-old Ahmaud Arbery, a young black man who was just out jogging in a coastal South Georgia neighborhood. He was chased and gunned down by a white father and son, who claimed they were within citizen arrest and self-defense statutes. It took months before the two killers were charged with murder and aggravated assault. They were only arrested after a video showing Mr. Arbery's struggle went viral. The oldest perpetrator was a former investigator for the local District Attorney's office, and the State of Georgia took four months to determine whether or not Mr. Arbery's death was a crime.

On May 25, 2020, four Minneapolis police officers arrested and brutally suffocated 46-year-old George Floyd to death. One white officer was charged with second degree murder after video tapes showed the officer's knee on Mr. Floyd's neck for eight minutes and 46 seconds. The officer did not remove his knee even after Mr. Floyd lost consciousness and paramedics had arrived at the scene. The more serious charge was added to those of third-degree murder and second-degree manslaughter. The other three officers involved were charged with aiding and abetting second degree murder and abetting second degree manslaughter.

Protests and riots erupted throughout the country. Half of the states mobilized National Guard units. Americans were concurrently dealing with two pandemics. There were health and safety issues along with a most terrible menace influencing the very heart and soul of the country. Systemic racism, inequality and social justice had crossed in an erupting path and citizens of all nationalities were raising their voices. On June 4, 2020, all 50 states plus 18 countries participated in Black Lives Matter protests making it the largest in world history. One of the rally signs stated:

Treat Racism like Covid-19

1. Assume you have it
2. Listen to experts about it
3. Don't Spread it
4. Be willing to change your life to end it

As we have learned through the civil rights movements of the 1950's and 1960's, demonstrations are an important beginning point to increase awareness and build coalitions. It is still a long road to get through sustained grassroots organizing, shifts in cultural norms, real policy changes, new legislation and landmark legal cases. We have seen the first level of involvement where people take to the streets and announce that we are not taking it anymore, but the message has to reach our institutions, our schools, our employers, and our systems of government for real actions and permanent solutions. These typically have to be morally, ethically and politically motivated. Most importantly, we have to be personally vested as individuals and families. We have to be willing to examine our own prejudices, challenge our way of thinking and develop a genuine compassion for those with different circumstances than our own. These recent events have clearly demonstrated that we are not nearly as far along as we should be with understanding equality and embracing diversity.

It was not until 1954 that the Supreme Court ruled racial segregation in public schools was unconstitutional and protests began that effort for the Brown V. Board of Education ruling.

It took a year for the Supreme Court to rule against segregated public buses in 1955 after Rosa Parks refused to give up her seat to a white person in Montgomery, Alabama. Again, boycotts played a role in bringing attention to the issue.

Black and white protestors held sit-ins at diners across the South, and that eventually led to desegregation in 1960 of public places like Greensboro, North Carolina and Nashville, Tennessee.

In a historic decision, the Supreme Court ruled in June of 2020 that the 1964 Civil Rights Act protects gay, lesbian and transgender employees from discrimination based on sex. This effectively makes it illegal for businesses across the country to fire employees based on their sexual orientation or gender identity. Explicit state laws are still necessary, however, to protect the LGBTQ community in housing and public accommodations.

Rev. Martin Luther King gave his "I have a Dream" speech during a March on Washington for equality and justice in 1963. One of his prophetic quotes predicts that "the whirlwinds of revolt will continue to shake the foundations of our nation until the bright day of justice emerges." In a different address, Dr. King also said that "The ultimate measure of a man is not where he stands in moments of comfort and convenience, but where he stands at times of challenge and controversy." The Civil Rights Act was signed in 1964, but it took more work and protests for the Voting Rights Act of 1965 and the Fair Housing Act of 1968.

Professor Peter Levy is the author of "The Great Uprising: Race Riots in Urban America During the 1960's." He suggests that Americans, in fact the majority of them, were not supportive of the wave of civil rights reforms and that directly led them to vote Richard Nixon into the White House with a law and order agenda. Mr. Levy states, "A general unwillingness of the nation to commit itself to undoing a legacy of discrimination in the education, employment and justice system insured that systemic racism persisted." He goes yet a step further to write that many of the same issues from the 1960's remain unresolved.

Civil rights leader and U.S. Representative John Lewis agreed about the unresolved issues. Mr. Lewis was elected to Congress in 1986 and received the Presidential Medal of Freedom in 2011. He was arrested and assaulted many times in the fight for equality, including when he participated with the Freedom Riders as they challenged segregated facilities at interstate bus terminals in the south.

Mr. Lewis led some 600 peaceful demonstrators on a march in support of voting rights in the spring of 1965. As they attempted to cross the Edmund Pettus Bridge over the Alabama River, they were confronted by a large force of state troopers and deputies. The protestors were overrun by horses, and attacked by bullwhips and billy clubs. Mr. Lewis suffered a fractured skull and called on President Johnson to take action. Millions of Americans witnessed this event on television, which became known as "Bloody Sunday." Within 48 hours, demonstrations in support of the marchers took place in some 80 cities across the U.S. This heightened awareness is what contributed to the passage of the landmark Voting Rights Act in August of 1965.

Congressman Lewis passed away on July 17, 2020 and wrote an essay to be published on the day of his funeral. He said the last days and hours of his life were inspired by visiting the

Black Lives Matter Plaza in Washington. He wrote: "Millions of people motivated simply by human compassion laid down the burdens of division. Around the country and the world, you set aside race, class, age, language and nationality to demand respect for human dignity." Mr. Lewis emphasized that voting was the most powerful, nonviolent change agent and cautioned that we must use it because it is not guaranteed. He stated that the soul of America could be redeemed by getting into "good trouble, necessary trouble." He called upon each of us to learn the soul-wrenching, existential struggle that has been involved in history because the truth does not change and the answers worked out long ago would help find solutions to the challenges of our time.

Representative Lewis urged that we "continue to build union between movements stretching across the globe because we must put away our willingness to profit from the exploitation of others." He issued a final plea for this generation to overcome hate at last so that hope would finally triumph over violence, aggression and war. His encouraging words echoed the sentiment that ordinary people could have extraordinary vision. He exhibited this in his farewell by stating: "Though I may not be here with you, I urge you to answer the highest calling of your heart and stand up for what you truly believe. So I say to you, walk with the wind, brothers and sisters, and let the spirit of peace and the power of everlasting love be your guide."

As noted by Bill Clinton, Congressman Lewis left us all with marching orders. The former president suggested that Americans honor his request to: "Salute, suit up and march on."

Given the current events, we know that the labeling, stereotyping and racial profiling continues against African Americans. We are also aware that there has been a lack of police accountability in incidents involving the excessive use of force. Minneapolis has banned the use of chokeholds and neck restraints in arrests and officers are required to stop other officers using improper force. These are changes that other municipalities have adopted due to Mr. Floyd's death. However, state and federal lawmakers should also change the standard for when police can use deadly force. It is time to prohibit lethal force unless it is absolutely necessary. No-knock warrants, like the one that led to the death of Breonna Taylor in Louisville in March, should be banned. Congress should change the definition of criminal misconduct for police for violating constitutional rights and further hold officers liable for damages in civil lawsuits.

At a rally on June 7, 2020, Minneapolis City Council members announced plans to disband the police department and invest in community-led safety initiatives instead. Other locations, businesses and colleges are also considering abolishing or reducing police presence. New York City is moving funding from the NYPD to youth programs and social services. Within these efforts are important discussions about how to stop the criminalization of addiction, poverty and mental illness. The ACLU has suggested that civilian-led crisis intervention teams composed of highly trained professionals, including nurses, doctors, psychiatrists and social workers could respond to people who are suffering with a mental health issue, for example.

Law enforcement agencies across the country need to re-evaluate all their policies and practices, with an emphasis on modifying detainment and arrest procedures. In addition, advanced technology should be utilized for recruitment, hiring and monitoring of law enforcement officers so that those with anger management issues, previous investigations, suspensions and transfers due to brutality allegations and violations are easily identified. Officers should be required to complete regular bias, diversity, and sensitivity trainings, along with the use of de-escalation tactics. Many of our women and men in uniform are dedicated to serving and protecting with the best possible resources, so most would be open to positive change initiatives.

Law enforcement agencies could also partner with additional local nonprofits for continued education about a variety of topics to include homelessness, domestic violence, sexual assault, mental illness, substance abuse, homophobia and race relations. Grant opportunities should be provided at the local, state and federal levels to create curriculum development, space requirements, instruction time and facilitators. These measures would enhance community policing in some areas and perhaps encourage more citizens to be involved with reducing fear, building trust and problem solving for their own neighborhoods.

Regardless, there will certainly be a huge paradigm shift and new standards involving reform initiatives and accountability measures. The role, presence and responsibilities of police in America is evolving and will forever be different.

Likewise, employers need to use diversity and inclusion initiatives for more than compliance obligations. They should provide on-the-job opportunities for cross-cultural learning, mentoring and relationship building among employees. Companies can hire consulting firms to offer special workshops and open up dialogue on a consistent basis. All staff members should feel safe and connected to their colleagues through a commitment to fighting racism and discrimination wherever and however it exists.

Creating educational environments that reflect diversity, equity and justice should also be a top priority. There are many resources available to approach race, gender equality and bullying prevention. For example, the Southern Poverty Law Center offers the implementation of a teaching tolerance curriculum for K-12 students and anti-bias materials that include strategies to involve family and community members. There is also a self-assessment for educators to help them handle difficult conversations and responding to strong emotions.

Teachers know that each student brings unique experiences, strengths and ideas and they want children to know their cultural history and be prepared to embrace a diverse country. However, many teachers also have strict guidelines to follow, time constraints and limits on their creativity. In order to include information about diversity, administrators, school board members, parents and local residents have to be involved and in supportive relationships with teachers and students.

Alpha Kappa Alpha Sorority announced that the organization founded on the campus of Howard University by black collegiate women will provide scholarships to the daughter and granddaughters of George Floyd to attend an HBCU of their choosing. On the day Mr. Floyd was laid to rest, Texas Southern University also announced it would give a full scholarship to his daughter. Kanye West made a 2 million dollar donation to support the families of Breonna Taylor, Ahmaud Arbery and George Floyd, with a 529 education plan to fully cover college tuition for Mr. Floyd's daughter.

Mr. Floyd's family has filed a federal wrongful death lawsuit against the city of Minneapolis and the four police officers charged in his death, calling the tragedy part of a public health crisis that has disproportionally affected people of color the same way as the coronavirus pandemic. The lawsuit alleges that the city permitted a culture of racism and excessive force within the police department. According to USA today, the case will seek to set a precedent by making it "financially prohibitive for police to wrongfully kill marginalized people."

One of the most endearing moments was a viral video of Mr. Floyd's six-year-old daughter Gianna, when she smiled, raised her arms and announced, "Daddy changed the world!" Yes he did little one. Yes, he certainly did.

CHAPTER FOUR

Early Signs

In the summer of 1973, my sister and I were overjoyed at the news that we were moving to North Carolina. Mom and Dad built a home on the same property of my grandparents and great-grandmother. We could walk to Beech Mountain Elementary School and Dad even constructed a wooden staircase for us so we could maneuver one steep hill that led to a short path through the trees right to the school playground.

What commenced would be seven of the happiest years of childhood. Our weekends were filled with family cookouts, backyard softball, croquet and badminton. We had a wonderful, older distant cousin that taught us how to roller skate, even though the rink (and everything else) was a 30-minute drive away to the nearest town of Boone. We also had adoring aunts and uncles and spent the nights with them frequently. My dearest Aunt Brenda was the most fun, outgoing and attentive to me. She would always whisper in my ear and say that I was her favorite niece. We loved to watch any kind of movie together that was along the lines of slapstick comedy. In some regards, I was almost as close to her as my own Mom. There certainly were never any boring moments with Aunt Brenda. She was always energetic, upbeat and full of laughter.

During this time period, my sister and I had no idea that Mom and Dad were struggling financially. The western mountains were still a location of limited opportunities and low wages. Dad was working in the service department of a car dealership and Mom was a teaching assistant. She was also an excellent seamstress and made clothing, along with anything else that could be created on a sewing machine. There is a hysterical photograph of me in my room where my dress and headband match the exact fabric of the bedspread, curtains and table covering. All that is visible in the picture is the outline of my chubby face among a crowded, hunter green floral print pattern. Mom was quite the decorator and also perfected the art of hanging wallpaper. Those interior design skills would prove to serve her well in the future.

My sister and I were definitely catered to and it seemed that we got anything and everything we wanted. Our parents were not in the least concerned that I was a tomboy and my sister wanted to be a princess. Christmas and birthday gifts demonstrated our vastly differing interests. My sister would get Barbies and dollhouses and I would receive match-box cars and race tracks. Then, my sister would advance to any easy-bake oven and I got a BB-gun.

My favorite present of all time came on my 8th birthday. I was fascinated with motorcycles and my parents bought me a brand new mini-bike. That is one of the greatest memories. I had to be the most ecstatic 3rd grader on the planet when I saw that shiny, bright red Kawasaki 75. It had a 3-speed transmission with 4.2 HP at 6,500 rpm. Technically, the single cylinder, two-stroke engine was designed to be non-intimidating, but I ruled the wide open fields with maximum speed at every given opportunity. Aunt Brenda bought me a matching helmet, so I truly imagined that I was on my way to riding with the ranks of Evel Knievel. Perhaps I would become a popular daredevil and stunt performer just like Mr. Knievel.

It was also around this period that I began to take a sincere interest in sports, a passion that endured throughout my life. I was still an obese child, but had some early athletic ability. I remember going to my first basketball game and enjoying the half-time entertainment from the Grandfather Mountain Cloggers. It was also the first time I noticed how beautiful the dancers were.

Our close proximity to the school meant that I could actually hear the crowds of cheering fans on Friday nights and I decided that I wanted to become a star basketball player. Dad immediately installed the goal on the backside of the largest tobacco barn, and I had another obsession. The goal rim was set at exactly the regulation standard of 10 feet. There was no need to practice at a lesser height, according to Dad, because I needed to be prepared for what I would actually be facing on the court. I spent hours every day, shooting from all angles and distances until my hands would start to chafe. By the 6th grade, I was a normal weight and could easily keep pace with players two years ahead of me, so I was allowed to join the team early. The following year, we were the regional girls champions.

The year of 1979 also brought a challenging transition, as were separated for the first time as a family. Dad had to go out west to work on houses with his brother. It was a matter of dire financial circumstances that my sister and I remained clueless about. By the spring, Mom broke the devastating news to us that we would be moving to Wyoming permanently. I was in shock and bewilderment. What about our friends? What about my basketball career? I could not leave my teammates and I just had a new boyfriend. This was simply a cruel and bizarre plan that made no sense whatsoever. Initially, I was a stubborn

12-year-old on a mission to disrupt this idea by presenting other solutions. Couldn't Mom and Dad just visit each other? My sister, in a stance that would mirror our entire lives, took the news in a far less emotional fashion than I did. I cried, pleaded, pouted and threw mini pity parties. I even suggested that I could stay behind and live with my grandparents. I was convinced it would ruin my entire life.

Finally, Mom, in her calm and comforting resolve, took my sister and me by the hand and led us to the back bedroom. There the three of us kneeled to pray together and asked God if there were any way for another outcome. Mom said we had to have faith in God's will for us. How prolific that was then and now. It would be some forty years later before I would come to understand the importance of trusting God's will for my life. I also may have avoided, or at least been able to mitigate, so many problems had I followed my parent's examples. There were tough obstacles directly ahead and I would be entering a troubled adolescence in unknown territory.

My sister and I were completely fascinated by my uncle's ranch that first summer. There were real cowboys, horses to ride and rattlesnakes to avoid. It was a wide open landscape full of tumbleweed and miles upon miles of desert views. We thought there were actually more cattle than people in Wyoming, and that was just fine with us because we both loved wildlife. We enjoyed seeing all the antelope and buffalo herds, while visiting historic sites like the Oregon Trail ruts. It was like a huge adventure land for us, but we were not looking forward to beginning a new school.

When I entered Wheatland Junior High, I found that I was drastically behind academically, especially in Science and Math. Books would be my saving grace. Mom and Dad encouraged our reading and we were always allowed to have whatever literature was of interest to us. My reading comprehension skills had tested at the 12th grade level before we left North Carolina, so I was able to excel in English and Social Studies. I also played first string guard on the basketball team and joined the track squad. My sister adjusted fine, as well. Our southern accents proved to be a source of entertainment for both teachers and our classmates.

My first year of high school began with some minor hazing incidents like having petroleum jelly smeared through my hair and having my head shoved into a flushing toilet. Back in 1982, those were fondly known as "getting a swirly"

It was also at the age of 14 that I discovered alcohol for the first time and it was a most celebrated experience. I fully remember my first drink and the marvelous feeling of bold self-confidence. Specifically it was Amaretto, an overly-sweet, cherry-flavored liqueur. I thought it was the best thing I had ever tasted in my young life, and it would remain one of my favorites for several years. Of course, my first drink also turned into my initial solo intoxication. I was with a group of friends, but none of them appeared to be under the same influence that I was exhibiting. We were supposed to be working on a homecoming float after school. I was so drunk that I fell off the back of a flatbed truck and banged my head directly on the pavement. Of course, I was totally numb and felt absolutely nothing from the impact. Thus began my fascination with the effects of alcohol and my desire to indulge in it at every given opportunity.

My dreams of a glamourous basketball career were very short-lived. After scoring 30 points in one game, I was finally promoted to the 2nd string J.V. squad. My sophomore year, I fully expected to be playing varsity, but I could not understand the motivation tactics utilized by the three female coaches.

I was accustomed to encouragement and celebration on the court, so I found myself blindly unprepared for humiliation and group punishments. Running lines, stepping bleachers and yelling about mistakes were foreign methods of discipline to me. No coach had ever raised a voice unless it was to offer a compliment or cheer of enthusiasm. In my guard position, I was confident about my perimeter shooting abilities, so perhaps I was branded a show-off or a ball-hog. Whatever the reasons, I was either singled out for ridicule or my talents were completely ignored.

The militant environment, along with the time-wasting exercises and endless rantings were mentally exhausting. I just wanted to play basketball and scrimmage while working on real plays. How were we going to win any games when our practice sessions were devoted to listening to screaming about how we were not fast enough on defense or we were not blocking out enough or not passing the ball enough? We were constantly bombarded with jargon letting us know that we were not doing anything right. We were just a bunch of lazy slackers that could not even follow simple orders.

Eventually, I did develop a defiant attitude that ballooned into full-blown anger management issues. I was used to coaches who actually got out on the floor with us to guide and demonstrate by example. I was accustomed to coaches that actually knew how to play the game and were eager to illustrate techniques together with the team. Now, we were subjected to random and continual criticisms from the sidelines. I inherently despised their methods and distrusted their leadership abilities. This was probably evident since I didn't have a very good poker face either.

I was finally kicked off the team for saying, "come on" to my fellow teammates as we were instructed to run a play and

I dribbled the ball across the half-court line to see all four of them out of position. It could have been a learning moment, but it turned into an ugly shouting match with the head coach. I lost the argument and the last words from her mouth were, "You are out of here now!" It was totally embarrassing in front of everyone in the entire gymnasium. I stomped off to the locker room, where I threw my shoes around the room for several minutes and cried in an absolute rage. Later that same week, a varsity player approached me to suggest that I would be allowed back on the team if I personally went to apologize to the coach. I declined the invitation because I was stubborn, insolent and contemptuous. Besides, the incident was not my fault because she pushed me over the edge. That was my immature reasoning at the time.

If I had the opportunity today, I would still make an amends to her for the incident. I should have been more tolerant of her viewpoints and respectful of her opinions. Most importantly, I should have been willing to examine my own behaviors so that I could be more useful to my teammates. Actually, I also owe those ladies an eternal debt of gratitude because my departure from basketball forced me to pursue other interests in high school that would prove invaluable to my professional career.

My sister faced similar challenges in trying to find her niche in adolescence. She loved music and wanted desperately to fit in with the singing groups and theater club. She had a tremendously beautiful voice and could easily hit a wide range of notes. She could even belt out a song a cappella with brilliant clarity and rhythm. Doing superb in any of the talent shows, she desperately wanted to be a member of Rhapsody or the Entertainers. The music teacher had her limited favorite students, and my sister was not one them because "she was just not popular enough." This music teacher actually told my sister that to her face.

My sister did go on to be successful with music, although she was never afforded the opportunity to really invest herself fully to singing. She performed at weddings, family reunions and other special events. She even recorded her own C.D. with original material that should have gone all the way to Nashville, but her destiny was somewhat interrupted with matters of the heart. She married very young and had her children early in life. There were few regrets along this path, as my sister was an amazing mother and exceptionally devoted to her kids.

My sister and I always had part-time jobs because our parents encouraged us to develop as strong work ethic and pay our own way for extra activities. Dad was a warehouse supervisor at Basin Electric Power Plant and Mom owned Allen Furniture. They were also in the process of building another house, so we temporarily lived in a crowded apartment. My sister worked for a local diner. I rode my bicycle to Day Light Donuts at 4:00 AM before school and then took an evening shift at the radio station from 4:00 until 10:00 PM three days a week. I absolutely adored broadcasting. It was exciting to read the live headlines as they printed off of an old Associated Press tele-type. Surprisingly, talking into a microphone was an easy task for me. It was exciting to pick out and announce music, while also entertaining others with a simple weather forecast.

In Wyoming, we were allowed to get a Farmer's Permit and drive at the age of 15. Mom and Dad let me use their bright gold 1970 Cadillac. It was nearly as long as a tractor trailer and literally got about 13 miles to the gallon. It was a plush vehicle and capable of hauling around a lot of people, but that hardly mattered since my friends could frequently be seen pushing it to the nearest gas station.

Of course, I mostly looked forward to weekend drinking escapades. It was effortless to get alcohol. An older lady at the radio station always bought it for me so I would not have to show up at parties empty-handed. I spent the night with friends whose parents had open minds and open liquor cabinets. We would also sneak booze into the drive-in movie theater or drink by a large bon fire at the lake. Mom and Dad would have allowed me to experiment with alcohol as long as I stayed in the house, but they were disgusted by dishonesty and worried that I lied about where I was going and who I was hanging out with. My sister did take our parents up on the offer to explore drinking and she got so sick on cinnamon schnapps that she had no interest in alcohol from that day forward.

By my junior year, the dichotomy in my personality had become a paradoxical amazement. I was truly a transformed mixture of Jekyll and Hyde. One the one hand, my grades were good and I was a successful member on the school newspaper and the yearbook staff. I was extremely productive on the Speech Team in original oratory. The topic was about my 18-year-old first cousin who had been killed by a drunk driver in 1983. The presentation was very persuasive and included statistics about the dangers of alcohol abuse, yet I saw absolutely no connection to my own current behaviors. There was a part of me that sought out deviant opportunities and I had developed a rebellious mindset toward authority figures. I even had distinct sub-set of friends. There were those who adhered to the highest standards of academic achievement and moral conduct. Then there was another group that thought challenging the hierarchy and breaking the rules was necessary in order to have a good time, so I began forging excuse notes from Mom so I could ditch classes and hang out with the rebels.

We would not always drink; sometimes it was a simple matter of going shopping or spending a long time eating out at a favorite restaurant. However, when my G.P.A. became threatened by a foreign language course, we (a misfit group of two girls and two boys) had to come up with a masterful plan. We were all failing Spanish together and our only hope was to ace the upcoming semester exam. With a trusting teacher who always pre-prepared all her tests, our mission was clear and strategic. Two would be stationed in the hallway, one would guard the classroom entrance and the final participant would break into the filing cabinet to get a copy of the exam. The entire operation went very smoothly in the quiet after-school hours.

The rough portion was understanding the questions, looking up all the answers and then trying to memorize them. None of us knew one word of Spanish. It was a class that we frequently elected to skip out on because it was right after the lunch break. We sat around with a case of beer and opened our books for the very first time. After several hours of intense effort, it was apparent that we would have to use cheat sheets anyway. One of the members of our clan actually took our copy of the test back to the school the day of the exam with the intent of sharing it among a few select others. This single act of misguided generosity would prove fatal to what otherwise would have been a perfectly executed ploy. All it took was one student, one exceptionally diligent straight-A student, to have a brief glance at the revolutionary "study guide" floating around the room and we were sunk. She went directly to the principal's office to report it right after class. What ensued in the following days was an intense investigation and a shock-wave of disbelief that rippled throughout the entire school district.

Two of us buckled under the pressure and two of us did not. I would not confirm the identity of my friends, but did not deny my own involvement. News of the offense traveled like wildfire and even reached the ears of school board members. There was talk of criminal charges, permanent expulsion, transferring us to the state educational facilities (known as reform schools), and imposing some sort of public humiliation as an example to other students that cheating would not be tolerated.

The worst part was waiting for an administrative verdict on our punishment. Finally, our parents collectively intervened and it was agreed that we would all receive a zero on the exam and apologize individually to the teacher. However, I was handed an extra mandate and that was to see a psychologist on a weekly basis. I did not understand then why I was the only one who had to endure counseling sessions. We were all desperate, we all got busted and we all said we were sorry. Mom and Dad offered little explanation about it and just told me to go and cooperate with any recommendations. Thus began my introduction into the mental health system, with never any mention of mental illness.

I did not look forward to sharing anything with this psychologist. She mostly gave me mini pep-talks about my talents and how important it was to prepare for the future through discontinuing any more immature escapades. I avoided regular questions about drinking and my sexual orientation because I did not think those things were relevant to my ultimate purpose in life, which was to make others laugh and have a fun time. Her obsession with underage drinking led me to write a full front page article for the school newspaper about teenage alcoholism. Again, I saw no comparison with my own situation because I was not partying with my friends on a regular basis anymore.

By my senior year, I had slightly matured enough to try and make some plans for leaving high school. I also met Father Kale at the donut shop and started asking him some questions about his views. He was a fascinating man and had a calm, patient demeanor. This was after many conversations with the Mormons and Jehovah Witnesses. I had listened extensively to representatives of both of those religions and admired their convictions. It was just that I would probably not fit in due to the many requirements. Mom and Dad afforded us a lot of freedom with exploring churches. They were most concerned that we were good people and believed in Jesus. My sister and I went to different places of worship with some of our friends on Sundays. I decided to join the Episcopalian faith and took confirmation classes with Father Kale.

Despite my sketchy discipline record, I managed to be accepted to the Coast Guard Academy and also had an Army enlistment promise to study communications with a shot at getting into West Point. Dad definitely wanted me to go into the military, but Mom had some reservations. She was afraid they would send me home on a bus with a pink slip pinned to my uniform that said: "Cannot adjust." I made my decision based on reading the book *The Lords of Discipline*, which outlined a brutal culture of hazing and abuse. I didn't think that environment would exactly go well with my personality. So, logically, I opted to accept scholarships to a small community college instead.

High school graduation night was a fantastic event because my Grandma Marshall had flown in from Pennsylvania and my Grandpa Ward flew in from North Carolina with my Aunt Margie. It was a surprise visit for me and the best gift I could have ever received.

CHAPTER FIVE

Seeking Truth

Dad was a person of few words, but when he did have something to say, he certainly commanded everyone's attention. He was also known for having a short temper at times, but this was usually directed at inanimate objects, like a piece of building material or a household appliance that was not working correctly.

He was the one that drove me for the first time, along with my overstock of personal items, to Central Wyoming College in Riverton. The only advice he offered was to "stay off the grass." I thought he was telling me to avoid marijuana, but he literally meant that I should always take the sidewalks across campus.

Dad was most famous for his sharp, three-word answer to almost any dilemma. It didn't matter how emotional or dramatic the issue at hand may have been, his response was always, "Get another job." In other words, doing more work would solve any situation and he and Mom certainly believed in staying busy at all times. Mom even got her real estate license while she was still operating the furniture store business. They were always remodeling, redecorating, building a garage or planning some other major home improvement project.

Mom typically handled any obstacle with a type of circular logic that we all had to pretend to understand. She would say things like, "Well, if there is a problem then there is a reason for the problem that probably is the problem and the problem is the reason so that still leaves us with a problem about the problem." These were the hysterical moments that often brought us together as a stronger family unit and allowed us to laugh when the storm clouds passed.

Alone in my dorm room, I already missed my Mom and Dad, along with worrying some about my "sistie." We had started calling each other that since the day we vowed to keep a secret about wrecking Mom's station wagon. It was a different sort of bond that we created around a particular incident and both of us kept our promise to one another.

Mostly, I did not want to disappoint my parents anymore. I spent a great deal of time grounded from using the car or seeing my friends. It was true that Mom and Dad held high expectations and rarely offered any compliments. However, they never wanted us to believe that we were better than anyone else or get a "big head" about any of our accomplishments. They had also always displayed such a loving example in all their devotion to each other. In fact, my sister and I were embarrassed all the time by their public displays of affection. Mom and Dad held hands wherever they went, kissed in restaurants and constantly spoke terms of endearment to one another. They never fought and rarely disagreed about anything, so there really was no dysfunction in our household and we should have been more grateful. Of course, deep down, I felt that I should get more attention and greater recognition. Now was my big chance. My voice could become famous and I might just rise up to ranks of a major network with enough practice and dedication.

I was immediately enthralled by the campus radio station and the public television station serving the entire state. I discovered quickly that I would rather be a serious news reporter than attempt developing a regular on-air personality. It was not that I lacked the sense of humor, I just had a greater fascination with creating story ideas and writing about current events. My first live breaking news coverage was on Tuesday, January 28th, 1986 when the space shuttle Challenger exploded. I remember how emotional I felt reading the details. It was ever more heartbreaking because of the teacher, Christa McAuliffe, who had been chosen for the mission. That day there was a heavy, shared sadness or strange type of emptiness in our studios. No one wanted to talk about it, or even speak to one another. KCWC-television continued coverage all day and it was the first time I realized how shocking and life-altering the real world of reporting could be and how my heart was influenced by having to announce the bad news of this tragedy. It was a lesson in humility that would have to be tempered with the realities of the job.

Our head broadcasting instructor was a talented and creative mentor. He challenged our critical thinking skills on a regular basis and was adamant about ethical conduct and objectivity. I would have to learn how to ask the most difficult questions while removing my personal feelings from the equation. With this goal in mind, he arranged several of the most difficult interviews imaginable with two of the most deranged and frightening individuals that I believed existed at the time. Of course, I tried to prepare with adequate background research, but I was still mortified.

I had to spend an absolutely grueling hour on the telephone with Anton LeVay, the founder of the Satanic Church. In 1987, he was already famous for writing a satanic bible and a book about occult rituals. I remember that he had a deep, resonating voice and slightly over enunciated some of his words. He spoke very slowly and was, at least initially, charming and polite, as I am sure most devil worshipers are with beginning introductions. Unfortunately, he also presented as intelligent, articulate and clever.

My professor was right by my side feverishly writing notes, attempting to assist me, but Le Vay just calmly explained how the world was full of stupid ingrates who invented morals and religions to create false hope. Further, we should all release our hatred on our enemies and others that deserved it so we could be cleansed of malignant emotions. He claimed the occult was based on the logic and indulgence in whatever was pleasurable. Greed, pride, envy, anger, gluttony, lust and sloth were encouraged for physical and mental gratification. Le Vay pretty much ran away with the interview, but his words were full of venom with no prompting from me, so there would be plenty of sound bites to choose from. In radio, we called these "actualities", which just refers to audio sections or clips that are added for credibility during the story. It did turn out to be quite a storyline, but he failed to have much of an impression on the student body. Most of my friends actually poked fun at it and some wondered what hallucinogenic drugs he was on. I should have asked that question specifically, according to my fellow broadcasting buddies.

My next daunting assignment would be even more demanding and required a lot of preparation for me mentally. It was an encounter that I prayed would go quickly without evoking the obvious contempt that I held. The Ku Klux Klan was on the march in the 1980's and there were headlines about Neo-Nazi and Klan gatherings with outbreaks of violence between racists and counter-demonstrators. There had been a wave of cross burnings across the country, along with increasing attacks on synagogues and reports that Klan membership was on the rise.

By 1985, there were allegations that the KKK was becoming more aggressive and was promoting a race war instead of segregation. My mission was to find out what was going on directly from the Grand Wizard of the Klan himself. He was very forthcoming about the goal to turn America back into a white, Christian nation by any means necessary. The Klan was on a godly crusade to save the country from drugs, mixing races, immigration and homosexuality. He also bragged that their secret membership included some very important people like doctors, lawyers and politicians. So, once again the story package put itself together through sound bites. It was an investigative interview, but all I had to do was read the questions I had asked and play his responses. He sounded exactly like the delusional, arrogant, insulting, enraged white supremacist that he was. Part of me wondered why we were even giving him the air time.

I also figured out what these leaders had in common. They held completely opposing practicing faiths, yet there was an encompassing void in tolerance for others. They also shared a complete lack of compassion for humanity. They were both advocates for violence and revenge against anyone challenging their principles, and perpetrated crimes under the guise of religion.

These memories caused me to consider whether or not some were approaching the slippery slope of this type of ideology again with the current situation and moving toward irrational and affective conflicts. I wonder, for example, why those protesting the Covid-19 stay-at-home directives are more heavily armed than the KKK of the 1980's and why it is necessary to purchase more guns in the midst of a public health crisis. I also ponder how Nazi symbolism is synonymous with American patriotism and why the Nazi, confederate and American flags can be seen together at some protest rallies. Apparently, some participating in demonstrations have no idea about what it might be like to be truly oppressed, as there are signs stating things like: "I need a haircut" and "Let my people golf."

A great concern is the possibility of a group identity that provokes a division of the "us" vs. "them" mentality. History clearly demonstrates how dehumanization can place "them" outside of the realm of moral obligation to enable and justify violence against "them." It is important to remember that Covid-19 has placed us all in uncertainty and anxiety. Again, we can look into the past and see that controversy always surrounds the opposing elements of civil liberties verses the common good.

I certainly do not wish to label or categorize all individual protestors because I believe that most of them are misinformed and misled. There are good, decent, hard-working people struggling financially that have lost their source of income. There are those that do not understand or do not believe the inherent risks of this spreading disease. There are those that are truly frightened that the government is trying to take away their freedoms.

One problem is that it is basic human nature for each of us to have, or search for, a source to blame for our suffering. When any catastrophe strikes, we automatically question the how and the why. Anything is easier to accept if we can identify a clear cause, but often times when we cannot, we create something or someone to become the target of our sorrow, rage and frustration.

Psychologists have suggested that we have "motivated perception", which is the tendency to see exactly what we want to see. They also say that we have "confirmation bias", which means seeking out and paying attention to the views that support our pre-existing beliefs.

There have also been numerous studies about why some may respond positively to bigoted statements and divisive rhetoric. These theories attempt to explain how psychological conditions are created motivating individuals to join hate or extremist groups, participate in offensive actions towards others, or support authoritative, suppressive and judgmental ideologies. One factor is that people become misinformed and are completely unaware that they are misinformed, which creates a double burden. Some feel validated by hostile and vindictive behaviors, while others are rebellious and want to introduce chaos into political and social systems.

Experts also say that Terror Management Theory reminds people of their own mortality and they will act out more aggressively towards those who do not share their worldviews and national or ethnic identity. Fear mongering might portray or label certain individuals as imminent dangers and can cause people to abandon rational, logical thinking to create hysteria and panic. Therefore, people may follow a leader, public figure or politician because they have become convinced of imaginary threats and believe they have found their protector. Hitler was a mastermind of fear mongering and propaganda, for example, and was able to create a "collective delusion" among an entire nation of people. It is interesting to note that, following the war, most Germans denied having any loyalty to the Nazi movement. According to historians, many others claimed they did not know what went on because they did not wish to accept any responsibility for the things that happened.

Are some Americans planning on alleging they did not know about the seriousness of the coronavirus pandemic?

Are others going to say that coercion forced their focus onto conspiracy theories and partisan politics instead of the public health crisis? Are certain U.S. citizens content with blaming the media for the lack of response? What are the excuses going to be from those failing to follow safety guidelines to stop the spread of Covid-19 and protect others? How will we accept accountability as a nation for the ongoing and future outcomes from the virus and blatant inequalities?

Regardless of the underlying dilemmas, we need to remain mindful that dealing with the virus will likely be a long process and coping with the aftermath will be even longer. A new study from the Well Being Trust warns us about "deaths of despair" from increases in suicide and substance abuse over the next decade due to unemployment, isolation and mental health problems. This is a heartbreaking prediction that will require a different approach to target special populations. For instance, our elderly residents have been trapped in nursing homes and assisted living centers for month after month with no contact from friends and relatives. Nurses report that this is causing "failure to thrive", loneliness and depression. Our older residents have been cut off from any outside activities and grandchildren or family members have to hold up signs and artwork through windows.

It is critical to prepare ourselves for a future that will not be going back "to the way things were." It is imperative to accept the realities unfolding and try to reach out to others while supporting efforts of unity in our responses. The quality of our lives depends upon our collective resiliency.

By my second year of college, I had been promoted to News Director and was in charge of morning and evening reports. I also had the opportunity to join the theater group and landed a leading role in Beth Henley's *Crimes of the Heart*, a comedy about three sisters in Mississippi. I was cast because

I could perform a perfect Southern accent. My parents and sister came to see the play. In the opening scene, I had to sing a lonely version of Happy Birthday to myself and sistie's laughter erupted throughout the auditorium. I recognized her cackling and nearly broke up myself in what was supposed to be a serious moment.

Overall, it was a very rewarding experience for me and I became very close to fellow cast members. Logically, we all drank together. I had a hard time remembering my lines during rehearsals due to frequent hang-overs.

It had not yet progressed to a daily habit, but my drinking did get worse in college and it was certainly the priority for every weekend. Wyoming was the last state in the nation to raise the drinking age from 19 to 21. As always, I had no problem finding someone to buy beer for me. There were plenty of older students and no one followed the college rules prohibiting alcohol on campus. There were also always parties going on in the surrounding areas. I rarely frequented the local bars because they had a reputation for a lot of fighting involving members of the Arapahoe and Shoshone tribes. Riverton was adjacent to the Wind River Indian Reservation. Every year, Central Wyoming College hosted a Pow Wow and it was an amazing spectacle to honor and celebrate Native American culture and history.

I graduated with honors in May of 1987 and eventually went to work for the state's most popular radio station, KTRS in Casper. I almost did not get the job because I was over-weight, which should not have mattered in radio. However, the previous News Director looked like a model and was more of a morning co-host as opposed to a serious journalist. I had to go on a public weight loss adventure with a national company, announcing my progress and promoting their products every day. It was a stressful and embarrassing process that ended badly when I developed gallbladder problems from the pre-packaged food.

I did keep some of the weight off, but I was already burned out at the young age of 22. The best part of the position was meeting so many famous people. This included members of rock bands, entertainers and politicians. Amy Grant was my favorite performer to see back stage because she seemed like a very spiritual and down-to-earth person. I also talked with Dick Cheney on a regular basis. He was a Wyoming congressman before he became Vice President of the United States.

With all the extra glamour of radio, I was still restless and missed my family in North Carolina. It was an impulsive decision, but I sold my furniture, packed up a few belongings in my Ford Ranger pick-up truck and headed East with 800 dollars to my name. Dad led the way for the trip, which covered 1,892 miles in a few days. It was October of 1989 and NC was still recovering from the remnants of Hurricane Hugo.

I initially went to live with my Aunt Kathleen. By this time, my favorite Aunt Brenda owned the Toyota of Boone dealership and the three of us had a marvelous time together. We were always shopping, going to restaurants, traveling or visiting with my grandparents.

Aunt Kathleen and I joined High Country Singles and the Ruritan Club for extra social activities. We also worked part-time for a wealthy Florida couple who spent their summers in Blowing Rock. It was excellent pay for light housekeeping and cooking duties. They were actually very entertaining and generous, so we enjoyed their company.

It was also during this time period that I dated the only man that I ever truly loved. We grew up together at Beech Mountain Elementary, and had stayed in contact via letters for the entire 10 years that I was in Wyoming. Honestly, he was probably one of the reasons that I wanted to come back home to the western North Carolina mountains. However, we allowed speculation and rumor to ruin our relationship. I still owe him an amends for having unrealistic behaviors and expectations. It is an apology that I can never extend because it could potentially cause him painful memories and more harm. I wish we could have remained friends.

Just as I was preparing to move to another town, I was blessed to be appointed News Director at WATA radio in Boone. It was an experience full of wonderful, kind people in a close-knit community of genuine Southern culture at its best. I worked hard at giving a voice to the people and always wanted interviews to be included in my regular newscasts.

Early on, I faced the greatest challenge of my broadcasting career. It was covering the brutal murder case of a 27-year-old Appalachian State University News Bureau employee. It was a most horrific crime that represented state-wide shock and outrage. She had been abducted during an early morning jogging route and was tortured, sexually assaulted and strangled to death. The perpetrator may have never been apprehended except that he continued looking for victims and next kidnapped an ASU student at gunpoint. She was also raped and sexually assaulted, but managed to escape from his car when he stopped at a gas station. She later explained to authorities that he had revealed to her the grisly details about the murder.

I had to honor to talk with her after these heinous crimes and she was the epitome of grace and courage. I was amazed by the tenacity and determination of this young woman, who was only an ASU junior at the time of her attack. Normally, her identity would not have been revealed, but she did not mind speaking out because she was going to be the key witness for the prosecution.

The murder trial was held in April of 1990 and I learned a lot about character and dignity from that process. Her testimony was stellar, calm and brave. She became a hero, and justifiably so. It was an overly emotional and heartbreaking ordeal. I again struggled with my own reaction of complete contempt while sitting in a courtroom so close to a vicious monster, who showed no hint of remorse. I felt sorry for the family members and friends who had to re-live the horror of losing their loved one. The prosecutor's closing remarks were a fiery account about the gruesome nature of the crimes and he asked the jury to show no mercy for this cold-blooded killer in handing down their verdict. It did not take long for the six women and six men on the panel to return a unanimous recommendation for the death penalty.

Following the trial, I immediately interviewed the murder victim's father and he said the death penalty decision did not bring him any comfort because "nothing would bring her back."

I remember this entire ordeal vividly, especially the pain and suffering on the faces of so many closely involved with the case. It was the first time I had to fight back my own tears while asking a question and holding a tape recorder. I would go on announcing the news, but with a heightened sense of awareness and sensitivity.

I recall losing my composure on air during another occasion while I was attempting to report the obituary of a dear friend. I had practiced reading it aloud by myself first and thought I could get through it. When the microphone went live, I could only start one sentence. I had to turn the mike off and on several times, stumbling with a slow rhythm on each word until I finally got to the details. It was obvious to listeners that I had a meltdown. The advertising director came running down the hallway to check on me.

I have certainly learned through my direct experiences that journalists are human too. They have a myriad of sentiments that have to be suppressed and hidden in the best interests of reporting the facts, no matter how horrendous the situation may be.

I cannot begin to imagine the frustration that members of the news media must be experiencing with the Covid-19 crisis. I think many have viewed the White House press room with trepidation and skepticism. Never in the history of America has there been such a malicious, intrusive and disrespectful attempt to completely discredit reporters. The past four years, our citizens have heard the term "fake news" and "lame-stream media" so much that they literally do not know what to believe. Now, during this international pandemic when accurate information is critical to survival, people, are quite predictably, not listening.

In my humble opinion, this has been a form of callous propaganda that has created the breeding ground for misinformation, conspiracy theories and outright delusional thinking. Individuals continue questioning the validity of scientists and public health officials. There are those who totally distrust the CDC and the World Health Organization. Social media remains loaded with ridiculous allegations, thoughtless memes and dangerous speculation.

First and foremost, journalists are bound by a code of conduct. The duty of the journalist is to seek truth and provide an impartial and comprehensive account of events and issues. Journalists from all media adhere to ethics to ensure reliability of reported information through honesty, objectivity, fairness, diligence and accountability. Professional integrity is the cornerstone of credibility and public enlightenment is the forerunner of justice and the foundation of our democracy.

Therefore, the overwhelming majority of reporters take this commitment very seriously and journalists all across America are not reporting false information or facts in a misleading way to give the wrong impression. "Fake news" is just a catchphrase that the public has heard over and over and over again.

Anyone concerned about news sources can visit Ad Fontes Media, which is an independent organization that analyzes news content using a rigorous, non-partisan methodology to rank media outlets for their overall reliability and bias. An interactive map is provided on their website at www.adfontesmedia.com with a scale ranging from the most extreme left to the most extreme right. For example, the Associated Press, ABC News, and NPR have high rankings for being neutral and balanced. CNN skews left while Fox News is hyper partisan right, according to the chart. All the major networks and print media are ranked for opinion content, extremism and fact reporting. This is an important resource so that we may become more informed about our choices for obtaining information and sort through the process of where to place our trust in journalism again.

CHAPTER SIX

Broken Emotions

By the fall of 1991, I decided to enter the enticing arena of politics. Having interviewed so many elected officials, I was confident in making a career change to work in state's capitol.

Before leaving WATA, I received a special award from the 1451ˢᵗ transportation unit for news coverage and reporting for Operation Desert Shield/Desert Storm. The group was stationed at Fort Bragg during the conflict and I maintained close contact with them so the folks back home would know about their assignments, progress and overall well-being. It was a recognition rarely given by the National Guard to a civilian, so I sincerely cherished the honor.

Becoming an education lobbyist offered a new realm of exposure and opportunity. I accepted a position to represent 3,500 non-certified office professionals in the public school, community college and university systems. A portion of my duties included traveling the state to present legislative workshops in different districts. One of the primary objectives was to include the membership in differentiated pay plans that were already afforded to teachers and administrators.

The position required diligent canvassing to build relationships and establish trust with those in charge. Collecting the signatures of legislators was no small or simple task. I joined efforts with the lobbyist for teacher assistants and together we wrote bills and proposed provisional language before the House Appropriations Committee. It was a delicate procedure to discover what might motivate some lawmakers. One senator signed onto a bill just because I told him that my mother's maiden name was the same as his. He asked me a lot of questions about my relatives and then reckoned they could have been distant cousins.

I was on a contract basis with my group, so I also worked for a marketing research firm when the General Assembly was not in session. Of course, there were always plenty of gala affairs, political events and receptions to attend with free-flowing alcohol and it was acceptable for anyone to drink in massive quantities without even being noticed. Typically, I ended up downing entire bottles of wine instead of having just a few drinks while mingling.

I had completed most of the agenda items within two years and, due to a change in the leadership of the association, I wanted to move on to new adventures. For the first time, I thought I might make a good attorney myself, but law school was not an option if I intended on supporting my lifestyle living in North Raleigh. I did have offers to join some lobbying firms, but I was not comfortable with the idea of representing multiple clients or specific causes that I did not personally believe in. Instead, I became the Manager of the Governor's One-on-One program. It was a mentorship initiative that matched youthful offenders with volunteers. The operation was interrupted with some state regulatory issues, so I reached out to some of my broadcasting contacts again.

One of my good friends from Wyoming made it all the way to a network and she actually got me an interview with

CNN radio in Atlanta. It was one of the most exhilarating encounters of my life. Just touring the studios, watching the live announcers and seeing the frantic activities in the control room was totally captivating. I did get to meet the Assistant News Director and he threw my air-check tape into a large shipping box underneath his desk that contained at least 400 other similar cassettes. He explained to me how many others had visions of grandeur about working at CNN. I knew he was not even going to listen to my recording, but it was still an amazing experience.

My friend is now Dean of Communications at a major college and is currently running for Congress from California. She did pretty well from starting out as a small-town reporter for K2 television in Casper, Wyoming.

I was not devastated by the notion of leaving broadcasting behind because I had already fallen in love with the world of nonprofits. I became Executive Director of a domestic violence and rape crisis network in Smithfield, NC. The program, known as Harbor, Inc., included a 24-hour crisis line, court advocacy, counseling, volunteer training and a shelter house. I worked with some of the most extraordinary women on the planet. My best friends from Wyoming, Andy and Keri, relocated to North Carolina and Keri came to work with me to create the Child Advocacy Project for Harbor. Andy and I had attended CWC together, so he naturally was in charge of master control operations at WRAL TV in Raleigh.

Harbor was certainly a stressful environment, but we worked diligently as a team to protect women and children. During my tenure, the program continued to expand services and we raised community awareness about the dangers of abusive relationships. Dearest June held the hands and the hearts of countless women as she assisted them with getting restraining orders, while also facilitating a support group for victims of sexual assault. In fact, she was named North Carolina's Victim Advocate of the Year, and we were certainly proud of our accomplishments in providing a safe haven for families in need.

The position of Shelter Coordinator was really the only area of continual concern for the organization. In fairness, it was an overly demanding title requiring constant supervision, individual support and arrangement for outside services benefiting clients. We struggled finding the right candidate willing to multi-task all these duties. The departure of one of our Shelter Coordinators in early 1997 was completely disastrous and I was solely responsible for mishandling the situation. I never had the opportunity to make an amends to her because there were legal issues involved. Over the years, I have often wished for the occasion to apologize to her.

Having been on the front lines in protecting families from violence and sexual assault at Harbor, it is difficult to know that people are now trapped with their abusers in desperate circumstances. Victim rights groups around the world report the number of people calling emergency hotlines and seeking shelters has more than doubled since the coronavirus outbreak. Most tragically, traffickers, who use force, fraud or coercion to make victims engage in labor or sexual exploitation, have new opportunities to commit more heinous crimes due to the pandemic.

Covid-19 has created extra hardships within an entire segment of those already marginalized and forgotten. In the midst of the public health crisis, potential victims of domestic violence, child abuse and human trafficking are at increasingly greater risk. Initially, lock-downs interfered with reporting incidents, avenues of escape for survivors and crisis intervention resources. Children are especially vulnerable due to spending more time on the Internet, possibly being unsupervised and the decreased opportunity for others to notice the signs of abuse (such as teachers and social workers).

The F.B.I. issued a warning back in March stating concern that school closings would place children with "unmoderated online access" where predators know kids can be reached. The agency has reported investigating exploitation cases in New York, for example, where victims are trafficked for sex and advertised as being "virus free" via online channels. Teenagers are susceptible to being lured in by predators on social media and dating websites. Social distancing isolates young people from their peers, mentors and supportive adults, placing them in possible danger.

By late June of 2020, the EU's law enforcement agency, Europol, disclosed that child pornography across Europe had increased 30% since the pandemic began. Cyber-traffickers are actually using webcams to livestream the sexual abuse of children while international agencies do not have the technology to investigate and hold offenders accountable.

NGO's and humanitarian organizations around the world have not been participating in anti-trafficking activities because the coronavirus has forced their efforts to address basic human needs like hunger and unemployment. Rescue operations and convicting traffickers has become almost non-existent in some areas leaving vulnerable groups helpless in other ways, according to the Global Protection Cluster. In certain countries, like India, girls and women forced or coerced into prostitution by their captors are now homeless and destitute due to brothels closing down and "red light districts" being abandoned.

In America, experts say it is important to note that victims are very rarely kidnapped or abducted by strangers.

Officials at the National Human Trafficking hotline report that youth are almost always "recruited, groomed or enticed" by someone they know. Grooming is the process where an offender manipulates, breaks down defenses, gains trust, maintains secrecy and then convinces victims to participate. Individuals most at risk of being targeting are runaways and those in low-income, unstable living conditions. This includes racial and ethnic minorities, LGBTQ minors and especially transgender people. Substance abuse and mental health issues are also risk factors.

Despite the conspiracy theories and misconceptions circulating on social media, there is absolutely no evidence that wearing a mask could lead to child sex trafficking. An investigative report by USA Today also determined that several celebrities, politicians and government officials have been falsely linked to human trafficking. The facts can be obtained from reliable sources like the National Center for Missing and Exploited Children, the U.S. Justice Department, the Crimes Against Children Research Center, the Polaris Project and the United Nations Office on Drugs and Crime.

It is relevant that different countries have various challenges in assisting victims and Covid-19 has presented additional obstacles. The descriptions and circumstances of modern-day slavery also vary throughout the globe. INTERPOL recently rescued mostly male victims from West Africa, for instance, after they had been recruited online and promised "decent work." Mainly women and children were rescued by INTERPOL in Southeast Asia after they were set to be transited by terrorists, as reported by the Office for Democratic Institutions and Human Rights.

By mid-August, marches and rallies began springing up around the U.S. for "Save the Children" events where participants report they are raising awareness about child trafficking. Organizers are part of Facebook groups, where millions of users have seen the conspiracy theories about an organized, secret, political faction of child abusers in government, entertainment and the media.

It is true that abusers are in positions of power and control over their victims. That has always been the case. It is also important to raise awareness about all forms of abuse, along with valid resources for prevention, intervention and direct assistance. However, the National Human Trafficking hotline has been overwhelmed with calls from people reporting a hidden trafficking conglomerate, asking questions about celebrities and making allegations against politicians. All of these inquiries, however well-intentioned, are crowding out calls from real victims. The real victims, according to hotline officials, are mostly concerned with food and housing assistance. Misinformation can also lead to donations for organizations that are not even serving victims.

The individuals disproportionately affected by the virus are also at the greatest risk for abuse and for the same reasons. In fact, those states with the most people testing positive for Covid-19 are the same states that the U.S. Department of Justice identifies as having the highest numbers of child trafficking cases to include California, New York, Texas and Florida.

There are 2,859 organizations in 199 countries addressing human trafficking listed on the Global Modern Slavery Directory. While this interactive and publically searchable database is a viable resource, it is alarming that many programs are facing financial difficulties and problems providing services to those in need due to the coronavirus.

The International Labor Organization states that human trafficking is one of the fastest-growing forms of illegal enterprise, generating over 150 billion dollars in unlawful profits every year. The ILO predicted back in 2017 that it would soon become the largest criminal industry in the world. Now, with the Covid-19 crisis pushing so many into poverty and increasing existing inequalities, there certainly should be a concern about having a pandemic within a pandemic within another pandemic.

By the mid 1990's, personal tragedy struck in my life that hampered my leadership skills and abilities to negotiate the formidable conditions at Harbor. These sorrows came seemingly back-to-back and set a series of life-altering events in motion. First, I lost my Grandma Ward around Christmas of 1994. Mom and Dad had moved in with my grandparents to care for them around the clock. It was a very strenuous obligation for my parents because grandma was in a wheelchair and my Pa Ward had Alzheimer's disease. He had to re-live the grief of my grandma's death over and over because he would often forget she was gone.

A few months later, Aunt Brenda was diagnosed with colon cancer in February. She kept her cheery disposition, keen sense of humor and positive outlook, but continued to decline physically. She withstood immeasurable anguish as the cancer metastasized to her liver and ran rampant throughout the rest of her body. I took long absences from work to spend as much time with her as possible. She was in and out of hospitals, while also enduring chemo-therapy and radiation treatments. I was unable to accept the unspeakable prognosis, even when she asked doctors at Duke University Medical Center what signs to expect near the end of her life. They told her that she would start coughing up blood and go into acute respiratory failure, being unable to breath, as the cancer had also spread to her lungs. I did not believe them and further wondered why they had done such an extensive surgery if there was no hope for her survival.

When Hospice was called into Aunt Brenda's home, she had been in agony for 10 long months, yet she never complained one single time about anything. In fact, she was always apologizing for being so sick and was constantly worried that she was being a burden. Even in the midst of her own severe discomfort, she tried to laugh and tell stories to console the rest of us. She refused to allow her pain to dampen the spirits of others. It was just a part of her caring and generous personality. She was never a person to entertain negativity of any sort, so she made certain that the topics of conversation were upbeat and encouraging.

In the early morning hours of November 2, 1995, we were summoned downstairs to my aunt's hospital bed. Aunt Kathleen had been crying by her side all night, gently rubbing her forehead with a damp washcloth. The Hospice nurse called a doctor for permission to administer a massive dosage of morphine. Aunt Brenda passed away peacefully while Mom held her hand and we stood in a circle around her. The nurse checked for a final heartbeat before announcing that she was gone. I ran from the scene screaming and fell to the floor in the living room. She was just 52 and I had lost my best friend.

People waited in line at the funeral home all the way out the door, through the parking lot and down the driveway to pay their final respects at my aunt's viewing. Everyone loved her and her influence would be greatly missed by many. It snowed the day of her funeral, just as we were leaving the crowded church. They were slow moving, enormous, feathery flakes that just lingered floating in the air. They were the largest flurries I had ever seen, yet they melted before touching the ground. It was though even nature, through the skies, acknowledged her loss. That Christmas, there were large, hand-cut snowflakes hanging perfectly in my parent's house. It must have taken Mom weeks to create these intricate paper designs. They were placed inches apart and covered the entire ceiling of the family room. I wasn't the only one to notice a sign from the heavens on that winter afternoon when we had to say goodbye.

After the somber holidays, I poured every ounce of myself into working harder for months on end. I was way behind in my obligations to Harbor, so I feverishly wrote grants and got more involved with community projects. I stayed busy with the women's council, United Way, the Jaycees, the Rotary Club and Young Democrats. Through all these extra activities, I was becoming more reclusive and distant from the staff and clients. I also had little interest in a personal life or doing things just for fun. I preferred to spend my weekends occupied with changing decorations in my home for no reason instead of going out and spending time with friends. I started buying useless household knick-knacks, running up credit cards and drinking beer after hours in my office. I lost weight, could not sleep well and was becoming easily agitated. I bought a brand new pick-up truck that I could not afford, but nothing made me happy and nothing was good enough. I even started yelling at my dog on a regular basis. My beloved Dalmatian, Oreo, could not do anything right anymore and neither could anyone else.

Finally, after I exploded in a fit of rage at the shelter with little provocation, I went to see a psychiatrist in October of 1996. He explained to me that it was approaching the year anniversary of my aunt's death and that I was suffering from depression and bereavement issues. I was placed on Paxil, an anti-depressant and Ambien, which was supposed to be a sleep aid. It is now known that Ambien is linked to behavioral changes, mood swings and possible hallucinations, but back then it was a popular sedative.

Over the next three months, my condition just worsened into full-blown paranoia. I became convinced that people were out to get me and ruin my career. I thought I was being followed by the government because cars with Virginia license tags were in the neighborhood. I was adamant that all the phones were tapped. My Harbor friends tried to intervene. They even crawled underneath my house in an effort to convince me that there was no extra wiring to be suspicious about. I believed there were hidden cameras everywhere and that I had no privacy. I put black electrical tape over my television and VCR controls because I didn't trust any of the indicator lights. With a knife and hammer, I completely dismantled all the telephones. There would be no more prank phone calls with just static or whispering on the other end of the line.

Typically, I sat up all night in a pitch black living room with a flashlight waiting for the intruders to make their next move. I watched for the slightest flicker or movement because I was determined to find all the clandestine listening and recording devices. I knew I was the target of something, I just did not know why. Somehow, I continued to perform my job duties in a limited capacity, but I was extremely guarded, irritable and suspicious.

At some point in the beginning of the New Year, my sister and her family moved in with me. I absolutely adored my two nieces and nephew, but even their presence was not enough to steady my personality. When sistie tried to ask me about my personal finances, I became livid and accused her of being in on the plot to destroy my life. I knew my bills were out of control, I just did not understand how it all happened.

My psychosis reached epic proportions on February 17th of 1997. It was my Grandma Ward's birthday and I decided that running away was my only option. I got into my truck and headed north toward Washington, D.C. I was tired, lonely and desperate. No one was who they said they were and, in my distorted mindset, I didn't even believe that Mom and Dad were my real parents. I did talk to them, but I was crying and could not explain why I was so irate and upset.

My sister had my cell phone traced and I had driven all the way to Richmond, Virginia. There I entered some random hospital emergency room to ask for assistance and then thought there was no safe place, so I should just continue to drive. For the first time in my life, I had suicidal ideation and wondered if I had the courage to just ram my vehicle full speed off the road. I watched for large trees that I could possibly run into, but then was distracted because I thought strange cars were following me and it could have been the F.B.I.

Finally, Dad begged me to turn around and come back because my Mom could not take anymore. He promised that no one was mad at me and no one was going to hurt me. That was the last call before my cell phone went out, but I told Dad I would return home. This had been an all day, 14-hour ordeal and it was dark when I stopped at a familiar convenience store on the edge to town to call my sister.

Sistie and Keri explained tried to explain to me that I was going into a hospital so I could feel better. It was a nice, private facility called Holly Hill in Raleigh. I had no clue that the two of them had involuntarily committed me, but I reluctantly agreed to ride in a police car. They followed me and then we were all in a big conference room at the facility with Dr. M.

They answered all the questions because I could not remember much and I certainly was not going to reveal that I didn't trust anyone.

It was nearly midnight by the time I was in a room and it was like I had been dropped off in hell. I just laid there and listened to other people shouting and screaming for help. I was exhausted and alone in a strange place.

CHAPTER SEVEN

Miracle Mind

Initially, I would slip my pills underneath the mattress until I was placed in a monitored room. There was a big camera with a huge plastic bulb and blinking red light placed directly on the ceiling over my bed. I thought finally it was nice to see a recording device that was not hidden. There was only one chance to swallow pills then, and the nurses were not very accustomed to waiting, so I was held down and forcefully injected with medication.

I would not get in the shower because I was afraid of being electrocuted and I would not eat the food because I was convinced it was poisoned. I figured out that snickers bars would be safe as long as I cut off both the ends.

There were some good people in this place with me and some very bad individuals as well. Some of them were not even people at all, and I was becoming intuitive at knowing the difference. There was one young man in his early 20's that I felt a certain kinship with. Although he could barely communicate at all, I sensed that he possessed a kind soul. His body was completely contorted, he had extreme difficulty walking and could only utter guttural sounds. His clothes were always disheveled and his head was extended upwards, but he always tried to nod in my direction and I thought he was very special. He had jet-black hair and the most radiant blue eyes I had ever seen. I encountered him every day and wondered why he was here.

Most nights, I felt like a trapped, caged animal consumed with fear about my impending demise. I was locked away with other frightened animals in a noisy circus of despair. I sensed that there must be a committee of some sort deciding my fate. I had no idea that I had so many enemies. Why had everyone turned against me and placed me in this terrible prison? I had no answers and was afraid to ask any questions.

During the daylight hours, I wandered the L-shaped hallway, went into the smoking room and laid in that miserable bed. I tried to read magazines, but the words looked like a garbled foreign language. I wanted to pray more, but I believed that even my thoughts were not private and I was convinced that I was confined in a mostly evil location. I wished I could help some of the others, especially around 3:00 AM when the screaming and the wailing was worse. I was too petrified to leave my room and investigate. I knew I would be punished somehow. The orderly's that came for the 3rd shift didn't really seem to care about people in the least, although their job was supposed to be providing for our comfort and safety. They laughed, told crude jokes and played cards, while just ignoring all the pitiful crying.

One afternoon, we were all gathered in the main sitting area for an art class and asked to draw a picture about our feelings. I penciled in a stick figure at the bottom of a massive hole, surrounded by mounds of dirt. Then, I drew a huge, extremely long, black ladder that reached well beyond the top and extended into a bright, purple landscape. When the instructor asked me about it, I told her that I would have something to keep me from being buried alive.

Two different counselors came to spend time with me, but I do not remember what they said and do not even recall the topic of their conversations. I absolutely dreaded to see Dr. M. He always seemed to just magically appear in odd locations at various different times. He had an extended, narrow and pointed beard, with thick glasses that rested near the tip of his nose. He seemed overly serious, but talked in a slow, monotone voice, while he fumbled through charts on his lap. I just did not like him and I thought he should be there in the overnight hours if he really wanted to know what was going on. Mostly, I could not even pay attention to his questions and the few I understood, I simply refused to answer. I still felt like a prisoner and I did not want to assist my captors in finding out any more information.

Finally, an outsider came in wearing gym clothes and carrying a basketball. This was something I could remember. It was almost a familiar, happy feeling, so I bolted toward the reception desk and just stood right next to her. She chose a group of about eight of us to get on the elevator with her and my anxiety was decreasing with every floor level we passed. I was allowed to go outside for the first time and play this sport that I loved so dearly.

The sun was shining brightly through a few fluffy clouds among clear skies. It was unseasonably warm for late February, so I was thankful to see nature again. I just breathed deeply and stared all around the facility before fixating my glance on the asphalt paved court. There was only one goal, but it was regulation height. We easily took turns at passing and shooting, eventually moving farther out from the perimeter for some wild attempts. I stayed mostly at the free-throw line and was proud to see that I could still swish the basket from that exact spot. Dad always said missing foul shots could cost you the entire ball game.

I didn't want to leave the court when it was time to go back inside. I was moving slowly at the back of the line and thought about running up a steep graded hill toward a group of trees. I knew we were at the very back of the building, but I could hear the traffic and view a small portion of the left side parking lot. If I could just make it to a main street, I would be fine. I could flag down a stranger or find a payphone. Someone would help, even though I was in a big city. In the alternative, they could just let me stay at the basketball court. These thoughts dwindled away as I obediently shuffled back onto the elevator. Besides, I could not disrespect this kind woman who picked me and trusted that I would follow the rules. She was one of the few good ones, and maybe even a dedicated volunteer.

Still, the taste of freedom sparked a new desire to the forefront of my delusional mind. I had no choice but to formulate an elaborate escape plan. It would take a lot of careful consideration and attention to detail, but I was determined to join the living environment again. I really did not want to go back home because I did not know who to trust there, but anyplace had to be better than this torture chamber.

I figured out that the first double room at the end of the hallway was always vacant because it was directly next to the staircase entrance. That door was unlocked only twice per day when a nurse came with medications. The time frame varied in the morning and late afternoon, but not by much. Over the next several days, I watched the oversized clock on the wall across from the reception desk and noted that the early nurse would arrive around 8:00AM with morning doses, while the evening nurse came close to 4:00PM. I had become compliant with taking pills because I did not want to draw any more negative attention and the forceful injections were painful.

Plus, I was quiet and withdrawn in general. I didn't talk to very many people, so no one would be keeping an eye on me or become suspicious.

I surveyed the hallway a few times and carefully slipped into the empty room. I had decided on the afternoon schedule because there were far too many people around during the morning shift change. I waited to hear the familiar buzzing sound from the opening door and bolted right past the nurse. I felt guilty that she lost the entire tray of medications, but I had to keep moving. By the time alarms went off throughout the building, I was down four flights of stairs and had encountered only one staff member. Unfortunately, I had to hit him in the groin area when he attempted to detain me and then I was in the main lobby area where I could see the huge sliding glass doors of the front entrance.

Suddenly, people were darting at me from all directions and I realized I was being assaulted by three men and two women. I viciously fought them and they individually would back away from me and then try another angle of attack. I was 5' 5" and weighed only about 130 pounds, but I was fueled with energized adrenaline and bursting with abnormal power. I could view the outside world, so my resistance was fierce. It was an extended battle, but finally they managed to secure both my arms and contained my legs. I was still flailing about on the elevator and all the way back down that dreaded hallway. It must have been quite a show for the fellow patients.

I ended up chained spread-eagle, face down to a mattress on the floor. I was forcefully injected several times, probably with sedatives and anti-psychotics. This was a dark and dirty room that looked like the walls were covered in blood stains. It was most likely another hallucination, but that is what I saw at the time. The ground was also oozing some terrible, thick liquid and there was an awful stench. The smell was so permeating and nauseating that I started gagging, while I forced back my tears.

I don't know how long I was there, but it was beyond terrifying in pitch blackness. There was no need to yell for help; no one would be coming and I was too weak to raise my voice anyway. It felt like the mattress was getting hotter and hotter, just like I was strapped into a large frying pan. I sobbed and begged God not to let me die this way. It was too humiliating and disgraceful. I had been beaten down by unknown enemies. After a while, I changed my mind and prayed to be taken on to heaven so my suffering would end. I was in engulfing agony, physically and mentally, so death did not seem so frightening anymore.

Somehow, I woke up in the middle of the night back in my room, but my wrists were still shackled to either side of the bed. I was dizzy and could not focus my eyes clearly. I saw the outline of a figure in the room and wondered if the devil really did make house calls. There was Dr. M. sitting in a corner chair just staring at me. He was motionless, with his arms folded tightly across his chest. He did not say anything at first and continued his uncomfortable glance. I did not speak either. Eventually, he tried to ask me about the incident. He wanted to know what happened, but I offered no response. He drilled me over and over to tell him what I was so afraid of. It was the same question at least eight or nine times until I screamed at him and said: "I don't know!" It was a truthful answer at the time and I was just so tired of fighting.

Long after Dr. M. left, I wondered why I could not hear the typical night time disruptions. The hallways were unusually barren and there were no signs or sounds from other patients. Soon I had my answer in a form I least expected. There in my doorway was the young man with severe developmental disabilities, except he was absolutely astonishing. He could not have been cured from his conditions, yet he was right in front of me as a powerful and peaceful presence. There was no shaking, contortion or unsteadiness. He stood straight, tall and silent, with a gentle smile on his face. He was nicely dressed and his hair was groomed perfectly. His deep, blue eyes were almost glowing with energy. I could not stop looking at him. I was just so enthralled and incredibly glad to see him.

He calmly clamped his hands together and spoke in an easy tone. "April, do not worry, you are going to be fine," he said. His voice was so clearly soft and comforting. I wondered how he even knew my name and why in the world he could talk at all now. It was simply impossible. I had seen him day after day and his predicament was permanent. When he repeated the same words to me again, I felt the tears well up in my eyes because then I knew. It was an overwhelming sense of peace that flooded my mind. I was positive, but I still had to ask him. I said, "You are not from here, are you?" He smiled again and slightly tilted his head to one side. His compassion for me radiated so brightly that it infiltrated my entire existence and nearly took my breath away. He answered me, "No, I am not from here." He was the miracle that I thought was never coming. How could I be worthy of such a heavenly visitation? My room darkened as soon as he left, but it was so silent that I could only distinguish the dim humming sound of a fluorescent lightbulb somewhere. My fellow residents were at ease this blessed night because an angel had made his rounds. I never saw him again.

Behind the scenes, a different type of war was raging between the facility and my parents. I had now been branded a violent, uncontrollable patient who had injured two staff members. They wanted me transferred out to the state mental hospital, the same place that housed those deemed criminally insane. Mom and Dad got an attorney and threatened to file a lawsuit. They thought I was too unstable to be moved and feared I might try to run away again.

Shortly after that, I had my own staff person around the clock. She sat in a chair directly outside the doorway of my room. She was a very sweet lady who was constantly asking me if I needed anything. She often brought magazines and even read some of the articles to me. She was nice to me and seemed to really care about my well-being. She would clasp my hand or gently touch my arm every time she was close to my bed. She became enraged one day when they decided to forcefully inject medications again and pleaded with them to give me some more time. She told them it was totally unnecessary and that I would listen to her. After that, there were no more needles and I took my pills whenever she asked me to.

Eventually, Mom and Dad were allowed to visit me. They were both really dressed up and that surprised me. Daddy's clothes always consisted of western shirts and blue jeans, but that day he was wearing a leather, western blazer. Dad got huge tears in his eyes and that shocked me too because I had never seen him cry before. Mom had to convince me to get cleaned up and then stood right next to the shower door with me. They brought me a bag of miniature snickers so I would not have to cut the ends off of the regular sized ones anymore. Mom always had a very approachable demeanor, so of course, some of the other patients were eager to talk with her.

Mom and Dad had to go through counseling sessions to prepare for my departure from the facility. Dr. M. was not optimistic about my recovery. I had the worst form of Bipolar Disorder and had not responded well or shown any improvement with the treatment plan. My parents were advised that they might have to become my long-term caretakers. I was to be supervised at all times because I was still suffering from psychosis and my behaviors were unpredictable.

One afternoon, Mom just showed up to get me. I had no idea I was leaving and really was not sure where I was going. I went to their home with Grandpa Ward. Poor Mom and Dad now had two invalids to watch over and we were both out of our minds.

My parents read every book possible about bipolar. One of their favorites is "A brilliant Madness" by Patty Duke. It is still one of the best available.

I was taking the anti-psychotic Zyprexa and Depakote as a mood stabilizer. I was also on some sort of Benzodiazepine for anxiety. For two months, I sat in a chair just sleeping and slobbering on myself. I had no motivation, no personality and no interest in anything.

It is strange how any other physical illness may have produced different responses. There probably would have been an outpouring of care and concern for my recovery. Then again, most certainly had no idea why I had just vanished. I did receive a lot of encouraging letters and books from my friend Jenna while I was staying with my parents, and it meant a lot to me. The Director of United Way sent regular get-well cards and Mom updated the ladies at Harbor. Keri took over the program, so they would be fine. Harbor continued to thrive under her leadership and we remained the dearest of friends.

Overall, I had been sick a total of eight months and Mom and Dad were tired of seeing me so pitiful, so they sought out another psychiatrist. Although I was able to drive myself to weekly therapy appointments, I was still wandering around like a zombie. The new doctor took me off of all the medications and started extended release Eskalith, which was the real form of lithium. Initially, I was on a higher dose of 450 mg. twice daily. It took just two weeks to work and by my 30th birthday in May, I had undergone a miraculous transformation. It was though something had finally flipped the light switch back on in my brain and I returned to my former self. The nightmare I was trapped in abruptly ended and I was so elated that I wanted to see my home in Smithfield. Travel was on my mind and I relished starting a new beginning.

My sister had taken over my house payments and I was grateful. She and her family wanted to stay there, but I did not. There were just too many painful memories and I did not see any avenue to re-connect myself to the community. I was also embarrassed of my mental illness and ashamed of my behaviors. I really had no desire to try and explain my long absence to anyone. Although I had to resign from Harbor, I was not financially devastated because we had disability insurance and I also received unemployment benefits. After everything I had been through, it seemed that pursuing a complete change would be in my best interests. I decided to further my education. This was a bold undertaking, given my limitations, but I was desperate to fight against this illness and accomplish something to make up for all the time that had been lost in my life.

CHAPTER EIGHT

Accepting Transitions

I filled out the paperwork to attend North Carolina Wesleyan College for Justice Studies. I would be entering the adult, evening program with two classes during the week and one of Saturdays. I had a wonderful academic advisor, but was still facing a tough curriculum.

By the end of the summer, I also knew that it was time to get back to work. I wanted to be busy again and re-direct my thoughts off of mental illness. I actually took on one of the worst jobs of my career, which was a live-in hotel manager position in Durham. I had to stay in a room with a loud beeper and a televised, front-door monitor. In addition to scheduling part-time staff, I was charged with overseeing ongoing renovations, handling reservations and typically pulling long hours behind the front desk. The only time off was spent in rush hour traffic trying to make it to Raleigh for my evening courses at Wesleyan. It was a miserable existence, and I found myself exhausted and frustrated.

My Grandpa Ward passed away while I was staying in the hotel. I was grateful that I had seen him in the hospital and had been able to tell him how much I loved him. An older black gentleman that I worked with saw me crying at my desk and spent a long time talking with me about how death should really be celebrated as a new beginning. We were not here to mourn, but to rejoice and carry forward the messages from our kin folk, as he explained. His name was Isaac and he was a man of few words. In fact, he rarely spoke to anyone. I will never forget how he bent down on one knee next to my office chair that sad day to offer his wisdom and comfort. We were practically strangers, yet he called me sister and told me about the legacy of his own family. I was both honored and relieved by his generous kindness. Soon, we were both laughing and sharing some humorous stories about our relatives. His words and actions gave me a fresh perspective at a period of real need and I often recall his uplifting words.

Eventually, one of my other co-workers told me about Duke University temporary services and I rushed down to their recruiting offices. After an initial application and typing test, I was called back for an orientation, which meant I was being accepted for placement. My assignment was staff assistant to the Director of the Sanford Institute of Public Policy. I could not have imagined a more prestigious and welcoming environment.

The university as a whole certainly held an Ivy League reputation with all its implications, but my experience at the institute was one of an encouraging, close-knit atmosphere of cooperation. All the faculty and staff were diligent in representing the best interests of students. I was anticipating an overly formal setting with rigid expectations. Instead, there was a peaceful comradery of mutual respect for individual talents. One of the professors there even volunteered extensive time to tutor me so I could pass statistics. It would be the only C grade I ever received in higher education, but it was celebrated as a magnificent accomplishment.

By 1999, I became the Graduate Program Coordinator for MPP students. It was a challenging and rewarding position, but I had my sights set on law school. I scored above average on the LSAT and had solid recommendations. Although I was wait-listed at most schools, I remained confident that I would get in somewhere. In addition, I was blessed to graduate magna cum laude from Wesleyan.

Beginning in January of 2000, a series of unexpected events occurred that would change the course of my life for the next 20 years. In my case, it started with a combination of bizarre weather and a unique personality.

Susie owned her owned her own computer store and made trips to Durham for parts and supplies. We met through a mutual friend and she offered to help with my desktop PC. Back then, it was a big deal to have a home computer and I was absolutely lacking in technological knowledge, despite the many training courses I had taken at Duke.

Susie was an outgoing, charming and generous person. She had a glowing personality full of laughter and boisterous, witty comments. We became immediate friends due to her exuberant spirit and my lack of a social life. I had concentrated on career and educational interests for so long that I had literally forgotten how to go out and enjoy other activities. We spent a lot of time at restaurants, bars and dance clubs getting to know one another.

When she first came to my home, she passed the truest test of all and that was being allowed through the front door by Oreo (My cantankerous, old, grouchy, people-hating Dalmatian). Oreo despised everyone and never wavered in her opinion. All outsiders received the same treatment that included barking, growling, snarling and showing her teeth. I knew I had to gate her in the kitchen or put her in the backyard for all visitors. Susie was the one and only exception. Oreo only briefly tilted her head, wagged her tail and then walked right up to her. Susie bent down to pet her and I was beyond flabbergasted. It was an amazing spectacle and certainly an incident I had never witnessed before. It convinced me that Susie was a special and genuine person.

The evening of Monday, January 24, 2000, snowfall started across the triangle, including Raleigh, Durham and Chapel Hill. It continued through the day Tuesday and set a winter storm record accumulating over 20 inches in a short period of time. I was blessed to never lose power, but transportation halted and businesses were paralyzed. Weather forecasters did not predict the devastation and had called for only about 3 inches of snow, so the area was not ready to respond. In fact, no one was prepared. The Raleigh-Durham airport had the deepest amount since measurements were first kept in the 1870's. Duke University closed down for only the second time in school history. The next time all campus activities were suspended was in March of 2020 due to the coronavirus.

Susie came immediately from Salisbury in her 4-wheel drive Jeep to rescue me and Oreo. She brought a massive amount of food and a ton of supplies. I was notorious for keeping a bare pantry and relying on fast food or take out at the time. It was three days before a gas station or grocery store could reopen with limited hours of operation. Susie saved the entire apartment complex and actually went door-to-door offering to take my neighbors to the store. They were grateful and word traveled quickly, so Susie was running a make-shift taxi service for a while. She would never accept any money from anyone and said she was just glad to help out. I continued to be impressed by her sincere concern for others and we grew closer over the next couple of months.

I talked to my Grandma Marshall on the telephone a few days before she passed away in March of 2000. As usual, she was upbeat and in good spirits. Towards the end of the conversation, she was even singing some of her favorite gospel songs. She had been such an inspiration for so many and her unwavering faith in God was an endearing example. I especially admired her willingness to always speak up for the disadvantaged, take a stand for the underprivileged, directly involve herself with political decisions and remain active in improving the conditions for her community. She certainly never had any fear in speaking her true opinions about decency, strong moral character and justice. She was committed to making a difference, even if it was not the popular thing to do and even if it placed her own social status at risk. These were qualities I certainly hoped to emulate.

I traveled with my parents to Pennsylvania for the funeral. Susie agreed to stay in my home to take care of Oreo. Then something surprising and amazing occurred. Mom and Dad suggested spending a few days in Durham with me after the trip. I called Susie in an absolute panic because they had never seen the apartment and I was worried the condition would not be anywhere close to their standards. Susie enlisted the help of a friend and the two of them spent three days cleaning, organizing and re-decorating. Mom and Dad thought the place was fine, but most importantly, they really liked Susie. That was a tremendous relief to me.

By springtime, I was ready to leave the Sanford Institute. Honestly, my new position was too demanding, even with all the support and assistance I had from friends and colleagues. It was a cheerful goodbye celebration and everyone signed a picture of the Institute that was framed for me. I sincerely loved many special people and students at Duke. It was a real learning experience that I will forever hold close to my heart.

Susie and I rented a nice home just outside of Winston-Salem, as I was looking forward to attending Wake Forest

University. The house was actually too big and I did not like being alone all the time. Naturally, my drinking became worse and I started having paranoid thoughts about the neighborhood. The commute was difficult for Susie and she really needed to be closer to her elderly mother and ailing brother.

Near the end of the summer, we agreed that I could postpone law school and move to Salisbury. I was content with the decision because my mental health had declined and the transition had not been a positive experience. Productivity was a vital part of avoiding depression for me, so I thought getting back into a team environment was essential. In addition, I did not realize how dependent Susie's family was on her for day-to-day necessities and activities. We briefly moved into a small house that was literally just around the corner from her mom and brother. This did not seem to make sense financially or practically, so we finally just went to live in her mother's home.

Susie's brother, Bobby, and I were truly kindred spirits and we immediately became very close to one another. He was a programming genius and developed his own rent-to-own software, along with managing a database of clients from home. He had a most contagious sense of humor and we loved to laugh about nonsensical things or debate current events from a different perspective. We shared a fascination with science fiction, outer space and the possibility of aliens. We were both devoted Star Trek fans, for instance, and joined with the opinion that the government was hiding information about UFO's.

Bobby was also a former park ranger who was devoted to preserving and enjoying our natural resources. Some of my fondest memories involve camping and hiking trips with Bobby and Susie. Of course, Bobby and I also had an obsession with alcohol, although neither of us would have called it that. Our discussions almost always included drinking. We were the first ones awake and it was not unusual for us to have a shot of liquor in our morning coffee together on the weekends.

In February of 2001, I became a Program Supervisor for the Guardian ad Litem initiative representing abused and neglected children in the court system. It was regulated under the auspices of the Administrative Office of the Courts for North Carolina, and I started out in a part-time capacity. Still, it was a state job with good benefits and the potential for advancement. I worked with two of the most caring and amazing women I had ever met in my life. Amy was the District Administrator and Linda was the Program Assistant. We became the three musketeers of advocacy, outreach and justice for youth and families across Rowan County.

We were remarkable together in our shared compassion and commitment to children in need. We recruited and trained outstanding community volunteers who were willing to go the extra mile to make sure every young person in the system had a safe and permanent home. We collaborated with social workers, foster parents and other service providers to ensure that kids had every possible resource that was in their best interest. Eventually, I was charged with reorganizing and providing support for the program in Cabarrus County. Although I did not receive a promotion, I have wished many times that I would have remained with them. It was a place where real rewards were realized in both reuniting families and creating new ones. It was a place of genuine devotion to others and those organizations are hard to find.

During my years at Guardian ad Litem, I also went to graduate school and decided to attend the University of Phoenix. Back then, online programs were not respected at all. The general consensus was that it was an easy curriculum or that one was not pursuing a real degree. UOP was much more difficult than any bricks and mortar school I had attended. I had to spend four to five hours a day on research, writing, team building and group projects. There were 37 students who entered the Master's Degree Program in Organizational Management and only four of us finished. I was very proud of the accomplishment and met a life-long friend on that journey.

My departure from the Guardian ad Litem Program culminated with a grand fan fair event that including doctors, lawyers and judges. My heart was warmed the most by the outpouring of gratitude from so many dedicated volunteers and community activists. It was indeed a special farewell celebration that Susie catered herself. She was a talented and creative culinary wizard who had a myriad of her own recipes, so the appetizers were another highlight for the party. Over the past six years, my influence had made a difference and I wanted to continue representing cases as I moved on to another professional realm.

In the time period with Guardian ad Litem, I also volunteered extensively with the AIDS Task Force writing grants, doing presentations for donors, working with board members and co-hosting fundraising events. The program provided social and medical services, testing, prevention, transportation, affordable housing and living assistance for clients. It was a cause I deeply cared about, as two of my closest friends were HIV positive. Even from 2000 to 2005, there was still a lot stigma, misinformation and discrimination that placed barriers for those needing assistance or seeking employment. This was especially the case in the more rural areas of North Carolina.

Currently, it is encouraging that AIDS research over the past three decades is actually assisting scientists and expediting the search for a coronavirus vaccine. Experts suggest that discoveries made about Covid-19 and HIV could be mutually beneficial due to knowledge about virology and immunology. Researchers are looking at antibody responses and how T-cell immunity kicks in, for example.

Dr. John Moore of Cornell Medicine says the duration of antibodies is critical because there are cases of individuals who survived Covid-19, tested negative for the virus and then were re-infected. The prediction is that a vaccine will be approved for mass use before the time period of protection is known, possibly requiring booster shots. However, there is also promising speculation that the fields of Covid-19 and HIV "are going to speak directly to each other." Viral suppression has been achieved through HIV medications and two, late-stage multinational HIV vaccine clinical trials are under way, according to the NIH.

In the interim of my professional career, Susie and I tried turning the old computer business into a location to sell used furniture. This was a misguided and even comical adventure that neither of us held much motivation to pursue. We were often stuck with cleaning junk out of old houses, taking items on consignment and a lot of heavy lifting. We also had to unload mini storage units that her mom owned because people often abandoned them. I always felt sorry for these individuals and would sort through photographs and other personal items for them. If we could locate owners or family members, we always returned what we could without asking for any back rent. There was no such thing as complete repossession of property in our minds.

In the spring of 2006, I became Executive Director of a partnership for education, and this was an initiative tied to the local chamber of commerce. I had a huge, fancy office downtown and lots of introductions, special events and "mini-meetings", as I called them. This was my term for chatting with important people in the absence of any substantial topic of conversation. I felt lost and disconnected in this unknown environment. There was a new Superintendent of Schools and that was the focus of attention for a brief period. There was also a huge board of directors, but no clear objectives or course of action.

In my brief period tenure, I wrote a position paper about the controversy surrounding the North Carolina educational lottery and completed some teacher surveys throughout the district. The mission was to enhance existing programs and encourage innovative teaching practices, yet there were few examples as to tangible results. This made me uncomfortable with my role, but I attributed the feelings to adjustment difficulties.

I became less responsive and noticed a level of anxiety and uncertainty that had eluded me for nine long years. Other than being overly nervous, I had little warning of the horrific attack that would entrap my existence again.

Mental illness was not a regular consideration for me whatsoever because lithium had kept the demons away and I had long forgotten the torturous circumstances of my psychiatric hospitalization. Then, I just woke up one Monday morning and was petrified of anything and everything. It was though my rational thoughts had disappeared overnight and I could not function. Fear invaded every corner of my mind and I was abruptly separated from any shred of reality. I was so frightened that I could not even cry or become angry about my predicament. In fact, I wanted to run away and hide out. I needed to be totally secluded and left alone to suffer in silence by myself. No one needed to know about the impending doom.

Susie and I went to see Dr. G. right away. He was semi-retired at Wake Forest Baptist Health and specialized in mood disorders. He was a kind, gentle and patient man. He had been my psychiatrist for many years and always tried to warn me that stress and trauma could trigger bipolar episodes. It was his opinion that I was taking on too much responsibility with my career choices and that leadership roles were especially demanding. He explained that it was not a question of intelligence, intellect or even determination, but a matter of consistency. Eventually, my illness would limit my ability to do things on a regular basis or adhere to strict schedules. Therefore, he was not surprised to see my condition. He mostly talked to Susie because he knew I was incapacitated and unable to focus.

Dr. G. placed me on the anti-psychotic Risperidone and prescribed Valium for my nerves. I heard him say that it might take a long while for me to feel better, and I was just praying it would not be like the last time. I would have to see him on a monthly basis until I stabilized, although Susie had his direct number if we needed him for anything.

The organization was generous to offer me a medical leave of absence with pay and I was grateful for this extension. I did have to resign after a total of only five months, but I was too sick to be embarrassed.

By the summer of 2006, I was still struggling and we moved into a rental house that Susie's mom owned in Spencer. Susie thought that the peaceful, quiet environment might help. Unfortunately, I developed agoraphobia and could not even leave the home initially. I was still having auditory and visual hallucinations. I was horrified to even peak through a window curtain into the outside world. I had to stop drinking because of the medications and eventually I garnered the courage to walk around Library Park, which was right through the front door. My legs were so uncoordinated and stiff. I had to stop myself over and over from counting my steps. Things easily became repetitive in my mind and then I had a hard time shutting them off. I started walking every day and ventured out a little farther each week. This was an extremely difficult task because I worried people were spying on me.

Overcoming the paranoia was a grueling process, and many days I wanted to give up. Then I would think about the Guardian Angel I saw in the hospital. There had to be others and I would have to find faith in divine protection. God was not allowing me to go through all this for no reason. He had a plan and a purpose and I would have to keep fighting against the bad days and the scary scenarios.

Although I was still shaky and lacking in self-confidence, I joined the Morgan Foundation as Executive Director in May of 2007 and literally had two weeks to pull together a charity golf tournament that was occurring exactly on my 40th birthday. The event was a grand success, mostly due to the easy-going nature of participants and the hard work of volunteers. Walter T. Morgan is a professional golfer who played on the Senior PGA tour and holds several Champions Tour records. The foundation sponsored The First Tee, which provides educational programs and life-enhancing values to youth through the game of golf.

Susie and I decided to move to Lake Norman so I could be close to my new job and we rented a wonderful apartment right on the water. At first, it seemed to a position where I could really utilize my skills in a fun environment. However, there were internal organizational issues involving board members, compliance problems and financial matters that presented constant stress. Susie was always by my side to help in the office or assist at the golf course, but even our combined efforts were not enough to stabilize the foundation.

Predictably, I declined into back-to-back episodes and starting drinking heavily. There was literally a short pathway that led directly from our home to a boat marina bar and that is where I stayed most of the time. Somehow, I managed to write grants and keep up with the paperwork, but eventually had to take Valium during the day to calm my nerves and function in a limited capacity.

Dr. G. placed me right back on an anti-psychotic and tried the anti-depressant Zoloft. Within a few weeks, I was in extreme bipolar mania and consuming even more alcohol, while working odd hours on too many projects at one time. The Zoloft had to go, but it took my Mom to stop the drinking this time. She called me and was very upset and angry. She told me I was under the influence every single time we talked and she was sick of it. If I wanted to drink until my voice was slurred, then I needed to just forget ever dialing her phone number again. That was devastating to me. I would rather endure anything than hurt my mother, so I quit that day and remained sober for a long while.

Eventually, I pulled out of the mental anguish again and was able to hire a wonderful Director of Golf. Mike helped the program to thrive and we are still good friends. Mr. and Mrs. Morgan were very generous in a lot of ways. Susie and I were treated to many VIP events and tournaments that we otherwise would have never been exposed to. We also met many famous golfers and became involved with NASCAR through Speedway Children's Charities.

In the fall of 2008, I went into another bipolar episode. Susie and I could not afford the lake apartment anymore and we had moved back to Spencer. She was working in a convenience store there, so this left me with a daily two-hour commute to the foundation and no extra help. We rarely even saw one another. In addition, the foundation had an entirely new board of directors and the chairman, a former Navy Admiral, advised Mr. and Mrs. Morgan to fire the existing staff. We all had to undergo evaluations with the Admiral to document a formal warning that would lead to termination of employment. My appraisal as Director was especially harsh and contributed to my instability. However, the actual program on the golf course was very successful. The kids were engaged and happy. In addition, scholarships were given to those families that could not afford registration fees, so I was proud to be a part of the accomplishments.

I received my dismissal letter just prior to Christmas. At least I could celebrate that I had lasted one and a half years, and that was longer than any of the other seven previous directors. Even in an altered state of depression, I was relieved that the burden of responsibility had been lifted.

When we saw Dr. G. in January of 2009, he asked me if I was finally ready to consider another plan for my life. I had been rapid cycling in a pattern of frequent battles with mania and depression for the past four years. My symptoms had been so severe that Dr. G. actually considered an alternate diagnosis of Schizoaffective Disorder at one point, which is a condition including schizophrenia and mood changes.

The family history was the final deciding factor. Two of my paternal uncles and one of my paternal aunts had Bipolar Disorder, yet they led mostly productive lives. My aunt was an R.N. and my uncle was the accomplished rancher and businessman that helped us originally relocate to Wyoming. My remaining uncle did struggle a lot more and underwent electroshock therapy in the 1960's. It is known today as electroconvulsive therapy. This involves sending an electrical current through the brain, deliberately triggering a seizure.

I think that he did suffer some memory loss from the treatments. I recall in his later years that he would repeat himself a lot and ask the same questions over and over.

I had to concede to Dr. G. that I was weary from the fear, panic and delusions that had consumed my thoughts for so long. Stress from employment had proven to be a constant trigger, so I reluctantly agreed to apply for disability benefits. Dr. G. tried to be encouraging, suggesting that there were many community projects and new hobbies that I could discover. Most importantly, this was the only way I was going to get better and possibly remain stable for a consistent period of time.

I wore my Aunt Brenda's long, black leather coat the day I went for the appointment at the local Social Security office. It was a way her spirit could be with me as I took this difficult step. They were prepared for the visit with my entire work history printed out on numerous sheets. It was sad to look through the pages. I hoped that I had made a positive impression for others along the way. I just had to verify everything and sign some paperwork. It was a shorter process than I expected, and I should have been elated, but I was not. My heart was heavy with both fond memories about the past and concerns about the future. I still was not ready to admit that I was entirely useless and that's what it felt like I was doing. There was a stubbornness and resiliency in me that had been buried for so long, but I did not have the energy to revive it.

Dr. G. must have presented a very convincing case, because my disability benefits were approved immediately in just three short months. Now I would focus only on my mental health and hopefully regain my full personality once again.

CHAPTER NINE

Faithful Memories

Running was never a natural instinct for me, nor was it even an area of interest, but I decided to push myself physically as a coping method. Although all the medications had worn down my defenses, the desire to overcome mental limitations was boiling ever more closely to the surface and, in brief lucid moments, I was having glimpses of my previous personality. Exercise was a way to release frustrations, revolt against fear and talk myself back into reality. I was no longer contributing in a professional environment, so I had to focus my efforts on accomplishing something else that would generate self-improvement. Portions of my emotional functioning and psychological perspective might be forever altered. At least that was a possibility that I had to consider. Gradually, I came to accept that these lost portions could be replaced by renewed possibilities. I would just have to adopt a "wait and pray" mindset with greater determination because past reminders of failures were unacceptable to me.

Eventually, I found what I called my miracle mile. It was a totally unpopulated, gravel road, quietly hidden away between the towns of Salisbury and Spencer. It was a mostly abandoned passageway that offered the freedom to envision a restored version of my mind and body. I started looking at my training as a blessed duty and inspiration for increasing stamina. Learning to trust my instincts and responses again was a process of discovery, and that meant the miracle mile was more than just another vision from creative imagination. It was a divine place providing hope, willpower and insight. While I was running, there was never any conscience thought about my limitations or future obstacles. However, there were many more challenges on the way.

As 2009 was drawing to a close, I received word that my dear friend Amy had breast cancer and the prognosis was not good. Amy had been so much more than my supervisor at Guardian ad Litem, she was my mentor, my role model and one of my heroes. She bravely attended her retirement party even after suffering through months of treatment that included brain surgery. Amy received the order of the long leaf pine, which is the highest award for North Carolina state service granted by the Office of the Governor. She certainly deserved that honor, as she was a true child advocate, dedicating all her efforts to families in need. I sent out a mass email about her strength of character, her devoted generosity and her kind leadership. Even in the midst of her terminal illness, she exhibited amazing courage and kept her thoughts on helping others. The entire process was so similar to losing my Aunt Brenda because I deeply loved and admired Amy. Following her death in April of 2010, I became more obsessed with training and running. That was the only ally I had to avoid another mental meltdown. I also rejoined the Episcopalian Church, finally completing my confirmation. This focus offered protection and progress in getting through the grieving process.

I strained myself day and night to develop a coordinated stride and faster movement. It started with sprinting down the miracle mile and then slowly moving along other markers to stretch out my route to four miles. I would jog shorter, uphill sections and then established other areas to alternate my pace with spurts of energy about three-tenths of every mile. I advanced to repeating the course twice a day, going once in the early morning and again in the mid- afternoon. Finally, I spent all day working out, with running in the morning, going to the gym to lift weights and then running again in the evening.

Somewhere along the way, fate collided with an adrenaline guided Eureka moment and the stories associated with my condition, hereditary issues or environmental factors faded into the background. I was developing more self-confidence and tenacity. Faith in running may have initiated as a survival technique, but it slowly advanced into an arena for lasting intervention.

In the fall of 2010, Susie and I were again moving back into her Mom's house. This time, I did not mind the transition because running was my new career and honestly, I loved Susie's family. Her mother, Mrs. Y., was a true Southern gentlewoman without any of the starch. She came from a wealthy family, but was never pretentious. She was educated, well-read and extremely talented. As a former music teacher, Mrs. Y. was absolutely amazing at playing the piano and enjoyed entertaining others whenever she was feeling up to it. She had adopted me as her third daughter and I called her Maxwell Mommy because we lived on Maxwell Street. Susie's sister Jeannie was a very spiritual, kind and encouraging person. She also always treated me like a member of the family.

Of course, dearest Bobby was the greatest gift of all. It was nice to return to our regular, off-beat and humorous conversations. I enjoyed his company and his insights on any imaginable topic. He truly was my best friend and most trusted confidant. Bobby had actually stopped drinking with his own faith-based method. This included writing various Bible verses on index cards and taping them to every cabinet, drawer, window pane and door. He also placed them all over his office furniture and in any location where he used to stash his liquor. It was good to see his resolve and calm, comforting personality. However, Bobby was never an unpleasant person, even when he was intoxicated. He was always boisterous and comical. His favorite phrase was, "I cannot take it!", which he would repeatedly shout out in laughter in his drinking days. Alcohol had still done a lot of damage to him. He suffered from chronic pancreatitis and had to be on high doses of Oxycodone for pain management. He was also on medications for COPD and asthma, eventually requiring him to go on portable oxygen.

Oreo never took a liking to Bobby and she constantly growled and barked at him whenever he entered the kitchen. On one hysterical occasion, Bobby decided that Susie and I were not strict enough with Oreo and insisted that he could teach her to respect him by taking her to the mailbox with him every day off of a leash. I had serious doubts about the plan because Oreo could be predatory and conniving. Susie and I watched from the back porch as Oreo calmly listened to Bobby's command and followed him all the way to the end of the driveway. The next door neighbor happened to be checking his mailbox at the same time. All of a sudden, Oreo started circling and showing her teeth before she lunged directly at Bobby's backside. Then she started darting around the yard like a wild bucking bronco. Bobby threw the letters in the air, bolted back toward the house and screamed out to the neighbor, "Run man run, she's not my dog!" Watching two men scramble while Oreo threatened to attack both of them was the best show we had seen in a long while. After that, there were no more attempts to educate Oreo in obedience or anything else. In fact, her status was elevated from grouchy and old to dangerous and unpredictable. Dr. G. always said that dogs get their personality traits from their owners and I was desperately hoping that theory was incorrect.

I was finally able to jog my entire four mile training route and thought I was ready for competition. On Saint Patrick's Day of 2011, I finished my first 5k event in around 33 minutes. I then decided to fill up my weekends with race opportunities because they brought excitement, purpose and a dedicated focus with uplifting experiences. I won my first medal at an 8k event in August. I finished 2nd place in my age category and was totally enthralled with racing. I increased my daily mileage to focus on endurance instead of speed, and continued to collect trophies and medals at all distances.

I also enjoyed a sense of mental and emotional stabilization that I had never experienced before, and it extended for several years. I decided to dedicate every race to the memory of a lost loved one. It was a special method to honor their legacy and I would have bibs printed with their picture for particular events. It was also rewarding that these outings raised funds for a variety of causes that were deeply close to my heart. In 2012, I set a track record at the Charlotte Motor Speedway for 40-45 year-olds. The Divas Half-Marathon was actually the highlight event where I celebrated my 45th birthday completing 13.1 miles in just over two hours. My PR for the 5k was a 23:45 finish on a paved, flat course greenway in late September. My toughest race was called a cool five and it is an annual event up on Beech Mountain, where Mom and Dad live. It is all uphill in a high altitude. I won first place in my age group, but it was a once in a lifetime challenge for me and I had no desire to repeat the course.

The first weekend in December, an incident occurred that threatened my life and certainly interrupted my progress mentally and physically. I had just completed an early route and was only one and a half blocks from home when I felt a sharp pain in my left leg. I looked down briefly and started to panic. I was surrounded by a large pack of pit bulls. They were biting, jumping and clawing at my entire body, trying to drag me to the ground. I was kicking, screaming and flailing my arms about wildly. I tried to move forward, but they kept grabbing different portions of my legs. It was Sunday morning, so the streets were almost completely silent. Finally, a passer-by honked the horn loudly and the dogs dispersed in various directions.

The onslaught must have lasted well over a minute, but it seemed like eternity to me. It was horrific and horrifying. I was wearing headphones, so I did not hear them coming. There was no warning. I was numb and in shock. I did not know where I was at and could not tell Susie on the telephone. My white compression socks were bright red with blood. I started to cry, but they were tears of absolute rage. I was more angry than I ever recall being in my lifetime. The ER doctor remarked that I was very fortunate to escape serious injury. I only had two deep puncture wounds on my upper left thigh. Animal control reported that I had been ambushed by five dogs and all of them had to be euthanized.

The psychological damage took a much greater toll. I changed my route for months and initially just did larger neighborhood circles because I was too frightened to be anywhere near Main Street. Eventually, I regained my confidence and thought it would be a good idea to be more involved with community activities.

By early 2013, I became a Head Coach for Girls on the Run, along with my good friend Jenn. I kept my promise from high school to be a different type of coach regarding motivation. I completed all activities, exercises and running with the girls. I never shouted orders from the sidelines; we did everything together as a team in an upbeat environment.

The program promotes empowerment by teaching life skills through lessons and running. I was blessed with the opportunity to work with a wonderful group of young ladies in 3rd through 5th grades. The Spring curriculum lasted four months, extending from February to May when all the girls completed a district-wide 5k event. I always bought extra things for each class session so the girls could hand out spirit awards to each other. These were simple items like stickers, wrist bands or colorful pencils. Whenever possible, I collected extra race bags from my events for the kids.

One season, Susie and I arranged for all the girls to have matching running shoes. Another time, they received sports watches. As a former paramedic, Susie volunteered to be our First Aid attendant. At the end of the program, we hosted a dinner and awards ceremony for the girls and their family members. Each child received a specialized, framed photo collage highlighting their participation and a large running trophy. These were special things that we did for our girls, but we had smaller classes than most other districts, so the children could receive more individualized attention.

In the summer of 2013, my beloved nephew James decided to move in with us. He went to work for the Food Lion warehouse and paid Mrs. Y. rent for the upstairs area of the house. Actually, Susie talked him into it because she was close to all my family members and especially cared about my sister's three children. Susie considered them her nieces and nephew as well. It was much later when I realized Susie was mostly a caregiver for everyone, and her life was consumed with attending to the needs of others. In all honesty, she also wanted James as a party buddy because she probably needed a diversion and wanted to have a good time.

The next door neighbors had a pool and an open invitation for nightly alcoholic escapades. Susie and James spent a lot of time with them in the evenings. They were a bad influence on my nephew, but Susie and I could have been better role models ourselves. I ventured across the fence sometimes too and my drinking certainly never stopped, it was only curbed back some because of my focus on running.

Bobby had experienced an especially rough year. He had several hospitalizations and even some extended rehabilitation stays in nursing homes. The worst event came when he experienced a mental breakdown and had to go into a psychiatric facility for several weeks. We all suspected that the combination of so many medications had caused the psychosis, so we were not prepared for the final word from doctors. Bobby was diagnosed with Bipolar 1. Needless to say, I was devastated for him. I intimately knew that internal trauma and was deeply saddened about the years he had lost without any treatment. An overwhelming grief engulfed me because here was a kind, generous and talented genius who had spent his entire life self-medicating with alcohol. He stabilized on Risperidone, as I had so many times. It was so relieving to have him back home. Somewhere, buried deep in my mind, I knew the interventions, all of them, were too late for Bobby. It still was not a conscious thought I was willing to accept.

When winter arrived, I joined the local homeless shelter as a volunteer. Taking the morning shift at a helping ministries from 5:00AM to 8:00AM meant that I could bring Bobby home a hot breakfast every day. I also enjoyed the generous staff and the thankful clients. Many of them were veterans, some were alcoholics or struggled with former drug addiction. Most were just without family members or friends willing to help them out for one reason or another. The organization had the assistance of local churches, restaurants and hotels in providing food and other supplies, so it was a collaborative and supportive experience. Susie and I also completed a pick-up and delivery schedule of donated items for the shelter.

By the spring of 2014, I was back on my strict training schedule and mapping out races that I wanted to complete for the year. Keeping a journal and calendar to record miles and plan specific special events was a priority. I always tried to register in advance because it offered me additional motivation. In addition, another successful season coaching with Girls on the Run was on the books. These rewards were hampered, however, by worry and concern for the people most important in my life.

I was still the first one awake with Bobby every morning to bring him his coffee. Gazing at all the awards and honors hanging over his hospital bed caused me to wonder how he managed to accomplish so many things. I remembered some of them because he had been my best friend for 14 years. As an amateur radio operator, he made certain we were all well connected during camping trips. I also recalled that he was a member of the FEMA crisis development and area intervention group and the community response team with the American Red Cross. He had exhibited such bravery against the odds, I thought.

Like his mother, he was a talented musician and could play the guitar or the banjo, and joined several bands in his youth. He was also a gifted carpenter and actually built his own home in the NC mountains. Everyone knew him as a trusted confidant. He had a special way to lend a helpful ear to individual concerns, even as his own health continued to dramatically decline. Mostly, I loved him for his caring nature and contagious optimism. I knew I could depend upon him for sound advice, encouragement and laughter.

Bobby was admitted to Hospice House in the early Fall and he was very content with the surroundings. Compared to hospitals and nursing homes, his room looked like a fancy hotel suite. The staff was overly warm and accommodating. The doctor told us she really did not have any distinct prognosis for Bobby, other than his lung conditions would continue to worsen. Although while he was there, he had shown signs of improvement. With little warning, the decision was made to move him back into a regular nursing home, where he would have to share a small space with another patient. I went with Susie when they transferred him and could sense that he was deeply disappointed, while attempting to act cheery about the adjustment. I touched his head, told him I loved him and let him know we would be back tomorrow to visit.

That night, I stayed up late listening to music in an attempt to fend off depression. My cell phone rang at 1:17 AM on October 5, 2014. It was a woman talking about Bobby and I thought she was calling to say they were going to move him again. I believed maybe he had fallen and they had to take him to the emergency room. She went on chatting for several minutes, but the point of the conversation was still lost for me. Finally, she indicated things were easier coming from a counselor. There was a pause and then she said, "Bobby passed away shortly after midnight." A million questions flew through my mind and I started asking them immediately. There was no initial grief, just confusion and frustration. I wanted to know how and why and where. Why would she call my telephone instead of any family numbers? The answers came too slowly for me. They did not know the actual time of death for certain because the nurses had just made their rounds. The cause of death was respiratory failure. My number was the one Bobby requested to be notified.

I walked down the hallway to Susie's room to wake her up. I grabbed her hand and gently pulled her from the bed. I said, "It's Bobby." She knew.

We were all amazed by the resolve and grace shown by Mrs. Y. There would only be a private memorial service at the home, as per Bobby's wishes. She asked me to stand at the front door to greet people and hand out mourning handkerchiefs. They were the old, linen variety with fancy embroidery around the edges. I did not realize this was a custom from the Victorian era. The formal areas looked wonderful with assorted flowers and plants, along with photographs and many of Bobby's special belongings. It was a nice tribute to his memory. I spent the next three nights sleeping on the living room floor. It made me feel closer to him.

CHAPTER TEN

Reality Strikes

Although I made it through the formalities of losing Bobby, the aftermath pushed me into emotional chaos. It was difficult spending our first Christmas without him. I dedicated a race to him in December and hung a large purple medal over the fireplace where his holiday stocking would have been displayed.

In the final months of the year, my drinking dramatically increased. It was so treacherous that I even started having a few beers before attending morning races, especially to battle tremors from the night before. I was also drinking and training, which was entirely dangerous. That was putting additional strain on my cardiovascular system, raising my blood pressure and increasing dehydration. It also meant that the recovery time for my muscles would be taking longer, but I had no concern for common sense considerations. I was just tired and lonely, so beer became the replacement for dealing with anything psychologically.

Susie had changed too and was also drinking a lot more, along with spending even a greater amount of time with the neighbors. We had grown apart and rarely spoke about anything significant. We certainly never discussed Bobby's death on anything other than a surface level. The grieving process must have been occurring very differently for the two of us. Susie was closed off and irritable, while I was aloof and depressed. I sensed I was going into another episode, but this time I had little motivation to do anything about it. Delusion and rebellion were sneaking into my behaviors again, which always signaled a shift in priorities.

On the last day of the year, I had the pathetic notion that I could celebrate Bobby by drinking Scotch all day because that was his favorite whiskey. Indulging in anything other than light beer was a very risky proposition for me that typically ended in some sort of dramatic personality change.

We always honored the Southern tradition of having pork, black-eyed peas and collard greens on New Year's Day for prosperity, good luck and health. I had also decided that I wanted Mimosas for breakfast, so that would have to be added to the grocery list.

New Year's Eve fell on a Wednesday that year and Susie had been gone most of the afternoon taking Mrs. Y. to a doctor's appointment. Later in the day, when I asked her to go to Food Lion, she refused. She was always the one to do the shopping because she enjoyed cooking and was particular about certain ingredients. In this case, she also knew that there were items that we had to have for the following day. I asked again several times and even pleaded with her, but she decided to remain stubborn. Susie had become mulish about a lot of things lately and when I heard the top of a can pop open, it was the sound of the beginning of her evening of drinking and the end of our conversation.

It was a frustrating predicament for me, especially since I was aware that I should not be driving. The grocery store was only two blocks away and she did not attempt to stop me when I told her where I was going shortly after 5:00 PM. I was all the way home and making the left-hand turn back into the driveway when everything came to a jarring halt. I just remember hearing a loud crashing noise, and feeling my forehead jerk forward to crack the windshield. I had taken my seatbelt off seconds before the impact. My small Nissan pick-up truck was completely demolished after being hit by a speeding Hummer. I was at a standstill and he was traveling at least 15 miles over the speed limit at about 45 miles per hour. The force of impact pushed the engine of my truck completely through the dashboard on the passenger side.

Susie came running down the driveway in her bare feet. I got out in a bad mood, but told her I was fine. I didn't notice any discomfort at first, and suggested to the driver of the Hummer that we should try to work things out ourselves. My truck only needed to be moved a few feet forward to be out of the roadway. Of course, there was not the slightest scratch on the huge tank that had just barreled over top of me. 911 had been contacted several times, according to the other driver. He seemed extremely nervous and naturally probably thought I was going to sue him. That was certainly the last thing on my mind at the time. I just wanted the entire ordeal to be over and done with. We could exchange numbers and deal with it later as far as I was concerned.

The neighbor saw the accident, and I tried to talk to her, but she did not want to be involved. I was exhausted and did not feel like waiting outside, so I went in the house to drink beer and take a nerve pill. After a long while, a headache began, along with some pain in my right ankle. I was still pretty numb, but had enough sense to know I needed to get to the hospital. I propped up my leg and continued guzzling beer for well over an hour before Susie came back inside and said an officer was on the scene. Where was the ambulance?, I wondered. The hospital was literally only three blocks away.

I was fumbling through my purse for my license when I approached the police. The officer just grabbed me, pushed me on the rear of his patrol car and handcuffed me. I was in total disbelief. I thought I was going to show I.D. and proof of insurance. He said I was being charged with driving while impaired. Trying to reach for my pocketbook, he asked me if I was resisting arrest. He then shoved me into the back seat and I still had no clue what was going on, but it was apparent that I needed medical assistance.

Once in the magistrate's office, I told him there was no probable cause for my arrest because I was in my home drinking for a long time after the accident. He had a lot of difficulty trying to convince the female magistrate to press charges. He wanted her to lock me up and set a bond. She denied those requests, probably because I had no criminal record. I did not refuse the breathalyzer because I knew that was an automatic DUI charge.

While he was filing the paperwork against me, I noticed that he was the chemical analyst specialist for the county. I did not think that was a coincidence. Is this what happens when a rich person is involved in an accident? Was the other driver important enough to make certain I was the one charged? That would explain why it took so long for anyone to respond. I thought this was the kind of thing that only happened in movies, but I was also paranoid and upset.

The incident report was worthless because it was basically a diagram of the street with the point of impact and did not show anyone at fault. In fairness, my field of perception would have been altered and I could have turned in front of the other driver. However, he was definitely speeding and not paying attention either because there were no skid marks. He made no attempt to brake. I investigated this driver myself and found out that he owned a car dealership and a towing company in a neighboring county.

The chemical analyst specialist officer continued to detain me long after I had been charged and should have been released on my own recognizance. He handcuffed me to a thick, wooden bar in the lobby and disappeared. I was there with a young black man and he was cursing and kept asking why he was under arrest. There were two other officers just standing around ignoring him. I finally tried to calm him down and told him everything was going to be fine. One of the officers abruptly turned on me and told me to be quiet because I was not allowed to talk to anyone else.

Within a few minutes, Susie and her nephew arrived. He was driving because she had been drinking beer and my entire family had already been informed that I was in jail for drunk driving.

By the time I was released from the hospital it was literally a new year. 2015 had certainly started off in the wrong direction. The ER doctor was a fellow runner and we talked about our favorite types of shoes. She was the only person who had been nice to me through this entire ordeal. I was extremely blessed, given the seriousness of the accident. The doctor told me my neck could have snapped, but I only had a broken nose, a soft-ball sized, swollen lump on my forehead and a small fracture in my right ankle. I would have to wear a boot cast on my foot, and dark sunglasses would be a necessity for months to cover my two black eyes.

We hired the best and most expensive attorneys available. I fully expected the case to be thrown out, even though I had blown several times over the NC legal limit. The question would be whether or not my blood alcohol level could have gone so high in a little over an hour drinking after the accident.

If that were the basis, then I could not go to trial because I would not lie under oath and testify that I had not been drinking all day. I still had a problem because there was no probable cause for my arrest. The case could have stopped at the magistrate's office and then it could have been dropped by the D.A.'s office. Then there was the suspicious lapse of time, the involvement by the chemical analyst specialist and the delay in medical treatment. I really did not have a solid course of action available, but I was still obsessed with the DUI charge.

I proceeded with taking the 40-hour outpatient treatment program that would be required if I were convicted. Remarkably, my drinking continued to progress and I resented participating in classes with "real criminals." Most of them were repeat offenders, with convictions that may have been completely separate from substance abuse. In the women's support group, I could relate to the story of one lady. She was employed cleaning office buildings at night and ran into a utility pole on her way home. She felt guilty and called in to report herself. A highway patrolman came to her home to record the details and she contacted her insurance company. She then drank some wine and nearly two hours later, a sheriff's department deputy came to her home and arrested her for DUI. I believed her story. She seemed like an honest, hardworking individual and she had never been in trouble for anything in her life.

In the meantime, my case was continued time and time again. That was part of the legal strategy and I was advised to commence with completing community service. This would all look better to the judge. I took an assignment at the local museum and was surprised that it was a wonderful place to work. I was fascinated with the history and the process for researching and archiving items. The director was brilliant and energetic. Eventually, she trusted me with more responsibilities and I learned a great deal. I actually would have continued to volunteer there, but she was planning on retiring.

I was also facing my third season as a Head Coach with Girls on the Run and had the embarrassing task of informing the district director about the charges against me. I was still allowed to coach as long as I was not actually convicted. Unfortunately, I did not do so well my final year with them. Susie had to fill in for me frequently because I was drinking and taking pain pills. The medication became a problem following the accident and continued because I was so frustrated with my ankle. I was unable to run and was sick of sitting around drinking while feeling sorry for myself.

One day, while I was still in the ankle boot, I decided I would paint the storage building deck and ended up falling through a rotten staircase, cracking several ribs on my upper left side. I was prescribed Oxycodone for months and months, with no way to get off of it. I did not tell my psychiatric doctors about any of this. Dr. G. had retired and I now saw someone different every couple of months. I was diagnosed with ADD and placed on Adderall. I was also given Ativan for anxiety and sleep assistance. I ended up abusing both of these medications as well, and would always run out of them before the end of the month.

By August of 2015, Susie and I were pretty much ignoring one another. I was drinking all the time and addicted to opioids. I was so desperate that I actually started buying pony kegs of beer, so I could sit them by the couch and refill my glass throughout the day without having to hobble to the kitchen to get individual bottles or cans. Susie was drinking every day too, but she started in the evenings and would usually go next door with the neighbors.

When Susie and I were not getting along, my sister came to pick me up and we went to Myrtle Beach to visit my oldest niece and her two daughters. Then we went to my parent's home, where I stayed for a few weeks. My drinking was dramatically reduced with Mom and Dad around. However, I was still on pain pills and was not being totally compliant with my bipolar medication.

Sometime in November, I was hospitalized because I thought I was going into cardiac arrest. I could not breathe after another bout with whiskey. Since I could not drive, I simply went out my back bedroom window and walked a short two miles to the liquor store. This time, it was alcohol poisoning and I was treated with intravenous fluids and oxygen therapy. However, I also had signs of pancreatitis. My poor Mom and Aunt Margie had to drive nearly three hours, with no notice, to get me. Uncharacteristically, I got into a fight with my Dad as soon as we were back in the mountains. He thought I was putting too much worry and stress on my Mom, and he was correct, but I was out of my mind again. I stayed several weeks and stabilized somewhat.

Upon returning to Salisbury in late December, I decided to skip Christmas with Susie and her family. I basically sat in the living room drinking, and it had advanced to malt liquor or beer with an outrageously high alcohol content. Honestly, I had a lot of unresolved feelings and blamed others for my situations. Deep down, I still thought the accident was Susie's fault. She should have gone to the grocery store. I was not thrilled that I had been gone for over a month and then there was the expectation that everything would just magically be fine. I tried to understand and I desperately worried about my loved ones in general, but I just felt lost and alone.

In February of 2016, I actually did a Super Bowl race in Charlotte. That year it was the Carolina Panthers versus the Denver Broncos. I was branded a huge traitor because I was pulling for the Broncos all the way. They were my favorite team from the Wyoming days, so I ran the course in my Denver attire. I had been off of pain medication for several weeks and thought I might have a chance at recovery. Then I had another round with my pancreas and was placed on Vicodin.

I tried to get back on track over the summer and actually took up cycling along with attempts to re-establish my running. I thought I could control my alcohol myself, but these plans always failed after a few weeks, so most times I was still drinking, taking Adderall and training. I could not stay sober long enough to enter any races and transgressed into another bipolar episode. This time, there was no psychosis, but a lot of fear and anxiety. My doctors at Wake Forest wrote a letter to my attorneys explaining that the stress from the DUI charge was an unreasonable burden that was worsening my mental condition.

A judge from another county heard my case because I previously worked for the court system. My attorneys successfully argued that I should not be required to appear in court due to mental illness. I hope it set a precedent, or at least served to raise the level of awareness. The lawyers entered a plea of guilty and I surrendered my license. I would be allowed driving privileges if I installed an ignition interlock system, also known as a "blow and go." I had purchased a nice, well-maintained used vehicle and did not want to go to the expense or hassle, so the car just sat in the driveway. The conviction was to never be listed on my criminal record.

It would take several years and divine intervention before I was able to accept full responsibility for my actions. There were many times that I had no business behind the wheel. I could have killed myself or someone else on numerous occasions, and I certainly needed to be held accountable for the accident and my behaviors afterwards. I wish the incident would have inspired a wake-up call in my conscience, but I revolted in further anger and denial instead. Alcohol and pills just fueled these negative emotions and I was oblivious to the steady decline in my mental health.

After the closure of the long legal trauma, Susie announced that she was having hip replacement surgery in September and did not trust me to be her caretaker. In fact, she did not even want me in the home during her recovery and had already made other arrangements with two of her friends. I would be welcome to return when she was feeling better. It was a justifiable stance given my circumstances, but I was void of any logical comprehension. I just felt abandoned and betrayed again. My life had evolved into a classic country music song. I was facing 50 years old and starting over again.

CHAPTER ELEVEN

Lost Purpose

When my sister came to drive my car and a few belongings to Mom and Dad's house, I did not have much to offer her in the way of explanations or excuses. A range of memories flooded throughout my mind and I wasn't really ready to discuss current feelings. Sistie was never hesitant in presenting her opinion. She thought Susie and I were incapable of supporting one another emotionally and that our relationship had become entirely dysfunctional. I was in no position to disagree with that assessment, nor did I honestly believe that my departure was temporary. There had been too many horrible things that had happened and, at some level, I knew I would not be going back to Maxwell Street. It was not a nurturing place anymore and was not in the best interests of anyone else either. I just was not willing to admit my own failures yet and did not want to pass judgements on other people.

My parents were undergoing major home renovations, so I would be moving into a chaotic environment. They were redoing the family room, kitchen and master bathroom. The noisy construction served as an extra irritant to everyone and I knew Mom and Dad would be particular about how the improvements were progressing. Of course, they were concerned about my issues, but never criticized me or asked any questions. The house project was actually a blessing because it was something that Mom and Dad enjoyed and could invest their energy into with actual positive results. I was not much help to them with any domestic duties, but was trying to better myself, so that was all that they expected from me.

I was so proud of my parents for all their volunteer work. They were active in efforts to restore the old Beech Mountain Elementary School into a community center. Mom served as the treasurer and they both were diligent about participating in the renovations. The center hosted a variety of family events, fundraisers and annual gatherings, such as the Harvest Festival. They accepted donations, offered a free clothing room and sold household items. The regular fish-fry dinners were very popular with the local residents, especially with the newly restored cafeteria. In fact, my nephew James was married at the community center. The location had been transformed into a beautiful retreat that could be utilized for group meetings, weddings and reunions.

I began walking and jogging again every day, making a pass by the community center as part of my usual route. Overall, my drinking was drastically reduced, however, I would often sneak around or hide alcohol in my room. Whenever my Adderall was refilled, I would stay up all night and drink. Dad didn't think there was anything wrong with having a few light beers, but Mom worried that any amount of alcohol interfered with my psychiatric medications. The generic versions of lithium carbonate had continued to decline in quality and did not appear to be of assistance with regulating my mood swings, so I did not take it very often.

I established another primary care physician and he placed me on a regular dose of Tramadol for my pancreatitis, which was far less severe than the heavier narcotics I had become accustomed to using. The expectation was that I would stop drinking because this was the obvious cure for long-term stability. I sincerely believed that I would be fine in a new environment with less stress where I could concentrate only on myself.

Finding a decent or affordable place to rent was nearly impossible because the area was still a college town and a popular destination for tourists, along with summer residents. As a real estate expert, Mom was insistent that I try to locate something that represented an investment. Eventually, we discovered a townhouse in Newland, NC at a reasonable price and I signed the final paperwork on Election Day of 2016 and recall the foreboding feelings. I moved in early and would be spending my first Christmas alone.

Initially, I was content with what I thought would represent my freedom and independence. I adopted the neighborhood black cat and named him Marley. Mom's older sister, my Aunt Betty, lived a few miles away and we spent a great deal of time together. We enjoyed going to thrift shops, traveling to nearby towns and eating at new restaurants. We had lunch together every Sunday and I even learned how to cook using a crock pot.

Susie and I remained close friends and talked on a regular basis. Although the dynamics of our relationship had changed, she was supportive of my new venture and tried to offer encouragement. After 17 years, certainly our families still loved and cared about one another. That was something that would forever be in place.

Overall, it didn't take long for the realities of home ownership to impede with constant aggravations. At least that was my impression of the situation. The guttering needed cleaned and repaired. I had plumbing problems with water leaks through the ceiling. The hot water heater malfunctioned and flooded out the crawl space, ruining all the insulation underneath the property. There was no homeowners association, which meant no maintenance of anything, including regular yard work. There were thermostat and electrical problems. I could barely afford to keep heat in the brutal winter time, let alone pay for repairs. The entire unit had to be re-wired for cable inside and outside, which was very costly. My water pipes stayed frozen and I had to spend days removing pine trees limbs from the parking lot after every storm.

I was thankful that insurance covered the damage to the crawl space and my former brother-in-law helped out a lot with updates. In addition, Susie brought one of her friends down to fix the plumbing damage. Actually, it was a blessed opportunity for me, but I complained and blew most things out of proportion. Again, I did not have my full mental capacities and was not prepared for the responsibilities.

Mom and Dad had also assisted me a great deal with getting into the townhouse and I was eternally grateful to them. I know they wanted me to thrive and become more self-sufficient. I just was not capable. There were too many interpersonal issues and addiction was at the top of the list, which made any forward motion in sanity an impossibility.

I found myself struggling financially all the time and could not manage my limited income whatsoever. Taking out loans and getting additional credit cards did not bother me because I was not thinking clearly about any repercussions. During one of my paranoid states, I ordered an alarm system with no thought as to how I was going to cover another monthly fee. There were three television sets that I did not use and an astronomical cable bill. I had every available channel, yet could seldom concentrate enough to watch anything.

I lived within walking distance of a grocery store and the Dollar General, which would have been ideal, except it was too convenient to buy alcohol every day. Any progress that I realized living with my parents quickly dissipated into a pattern of constant drinking. My attempts at moderating failed miserably. I tried only drinking in the late afternoons, limiting myself to a six pack of beer and then switching to wine. Eventually, craft beers with the highest alcohol content became my favorite and then I deteriorated to malt liquor because it was far more economical. I started missing birthdays, holidays, special events and all family gatherings. I was always too sick to attend anything and became completely self-absorbed.

I saw a different doctor for pancreatitis and he placed me right back on Oxycodone. He thought it was a better option than the Fentanyl patch. I also had a supply of hydrocodone due to severe dental problems. The pills would always run out and I would go through terrible withdrawal symptoms. I would drink even more massive quantities of alcohol when I did not have the pain medications.

Of course, prescription side-effects often intensified my frequent bouts with alcoholic blackouts. I fooled myself repeatedly into the notion that I could handle all circumstances and consistently manage everything in my life. In these darker moments, I pondered how the personal emotions and professional obligations were forever intertwining and ultimately admitted that figuring out the balance must be the task of saints or those with unique talents beyond my level of understanding. So, I was not concerned with trying to negotiate other personalities, relationships or contrary interests because drinking allowed my conscience to simply disappear. I did not know what was real or imagined in my own mind.

My brain was similar to a computer that does not respond when the memory becomes bogged down with too many requests at the same time.

I spent my time in isolation, content with talking to myself through intensified depression and self-pity. Worries about complicated disputes multiplied over the passing months and thoughts of previous mistakes ballooned into vast conspiracy theories. I had no control in monitoring the proportions about some of the most dreadful possibilities that entered my mind. I understood that logic was the best defense against fear, but emotional responses typically overshadowed any rational conclusions. Alcohol was the only remedy for removing myself from scary propositions, and I was not willing to give it up, even if it cost me my life. Coping with mental illness was enough of a challenge. I literally thought that I was entitled to drink because I was the victim of an unforgiving mood disorder.

My sister lived in Illinois during this time period and was horrified whenever she visited. She tried to have me admitted for in-patient treatment on three separate occasions but there were never any psychiatric beds available. One time I escaped from the ER room myself because there was potentially a three day hospital stay prior to be transferred for any type of substance abuse intervention. I simply went to the parking lot and called my Aunt Betty to come pick me up.

In another instance, my sister tried to get me into a program at a larger regional medical center and there was no help from that facility either. In a final act of desperation, she called my doctors at Wake Forest Baptist Health and threatened to sue them for keeping me on Adderall and Ativan. She told them I had a huge problem with alcohol and was abusing pain medications. She called them incompetent for failing to manage my Bipolar Disorder and suggested she was going to hold them legally liable for the decline in my condition.

Mom took me to my next appointment at Wake Forest and it was entirely accusatory and stressful for all involved parties. The Chief of Psychiatry was there holding stacks of folders and paperwork the equivalent of about three encyclopedias. She asked me if I was still smoking pot and I told her she had me confused with another patient. She persisted and wanted to know when I had stopped marijuana and what other street drugs I was using.

The expression on Mom's face was so alarming, that I actually worried she might pass out. Somewhere there was a notation that I admitted to "smoking", so I had to clarify tobacco products. The attending doctor intervened and started questioning me about my sister's allegations. I did not deny anything, but reported that I was not currently on any medications and that was the truth at that particular moment. I complied with their request for a drug screen, however, I was too dehydrated for the nurse to obtain a blood sample. The urinalysis came back as inconclusive. When we left, the only thing I had was a prescription for an antihistamine.

Mom was completely bewildered by the entire encounter. She wanted to know what type of mental health plan we had just experienced. I simply said it was the most interaction I had completed with anyone in years.

The significance of my deteriorating health was not something that I was able to fully understand because my motivation was lost and the focus was on a day-to-day routine that was void of any purpose or direction. I had come to define faith as a survival technique as opposed to any mechanism for personal advancement. This had more to do with unexpected challenges than it did with upbringing, formal education or direct experiences. Buried within the deepest realms of my tormented mindset was the notion that I probably did not even deserve to be stable to begin with. There had been too many offenses, too much psychological baggage and too many excuses. There was also an opposing portion of my personality that was not even open to acknowledging or comprehending responsibility for the lack of meaning in my life.

The only worthwhile endeavor that I accomplished was walking along the roadway a few times every week to pick garbage up along the ditch lines. Littering was the only thing that I could not tolerate. This was not an unusual phenomenon, as I grew up seeing my Dad perform this community service. It ended up being about a two-mile trek and sometimes people would actually stop and hand me their cans because they thought I was out collecting aluminum to bag and sell. Others would ask if I needed a ride somewhere. I must have looked pretty rough during these outings, but I had long stopped caring about my appearance.

In December of 2017, Susie and Mrs. Y. came to visit me and my Mom was there too, so it was one of the rare uplifting experiences. My Mom and Susie's Mom always admired, respected and loved one another. It was good to see them together again. Just after Christmas, Andy and Keri spent several nights with me and I was overjoyed with their company. It was hard to believe we had been dearest friends for 32 years and could still laugh about all the Wyoming escapades. Things seemed better in these brief interludes, with small moments of happiness.

I had endured two harsh winters and was finally off of opioids by the beginning of 2018. It was still bitterly cold with snow flurries accumulating well into spring time. Alcohol continued to be the top priority in my life and now I was drinking to the point of passing out every night. Taking a shower or doing laundry represented major achievements.

Mom tried to be supportive and encouraging. She called several times a day and would worry extensively if I did not answer. She visited often and took me shopping and out to eat. She never knew this, but I kept a little red notebook full of quotes from our conversations. Actually, I jotted down things often from telephone calls. It was an old habit from my journalism days that I never managed to alter. In Mom's case, it was a really good idea to remember what she said because she had a quick wit and some amazing insights. Many of them were inspiring to me. Once she commented: "We all need diversions and purpose because life can be real boring without them. Besides, interaction, even the frustrating kind, is better than doing nothing. Maybe you might accidently make a difference, change a life or create a positive future for someone else. Regardless, no one can label you with not trying."

Mom certainly sensed that I had become increasingly reclusive and distant. She knew that cutting myself off from the outside world was not healthy and that I was basically trapped wandering around in my own head. One another occasion, she said to me, "True perception is the knowledge that our problems never just appear. True faith is the knowledge that our problems will disappear." I cherished and respected her wisdom, but I was just too lost to fully internalize the meanings or respond with any motivation, so my decline continued unabated.

Sometime in mid-April, I sensed a pancreatic attack coming on. I had to quit eating and immediately stop the beer. I began taking heavy doses of Zofran, an anti-nausea medication, but it was not enough this time. Within 48 hours, I could not even keep water down and was vomiting up bile on a continual basis. It felt like I had been stabbed with a long knife through my upper abdomen that was protruding all the way out my back. My heart rate was extremely accelerated and then I had difficulty breathing. There was no time to call my aunt and make a casual trip to the ER. I knew my life was at risk. I notified 911 and explained the desperate circumstances. An ambulance was there in about three minutes. I was directly placed on oxygen, but the paramedics could not get an I.V. started.

The response was expedient at the hospital because there could have been bleeding, tissue damage, infection or harm to my heart, lungs and kidneys. Intravenous fluids were initiated to include morphine and antibiotics. I was whisked away for a CT scan and then placed in intensive care directly adjacent to the nurse's station, where all my vital signs could be constantly monitored. There was an alarm on my bed, so I could not even move without someone rushing into the room. I was dizzy, weak and exhausted, and mostly slept for several days. Eventually, I could keep down liquids and progressed to solid foods again. Everyone was very attentive and I received excellent care. Shockingly, there was little mention of alcohol abuse with the exception of an initial questionnaire by a nursing supervisor. A social worker visited to offer some information about community resources. It was a short list and I was certainly very aware of the limited options for mental health treatment.

I was released with a packet of paperwork about the medications that had been administered during my stay and diagramed documents about acute pancreatitis. The hospital made an appointment with yet another primary care physician and I was sent home with prescriptions for hydrocodone and Xanax. I saw the new doctor within a week and she referred me to a pain clinic. It was a 30-minute drive, so Mom took me to both appointments. There I was charged an outrageous amount for a small bottle of CBD oil and informed that smoking pot might be the best option for pain management, although medical marijuana was not legal in the state. Within a couple of weeks, I was right back to drinking again.

In the meantime, my sister had moved to Florida and when she visited me again, it was with a strict ultimatum. I could go into impatient treatment or live with her. Those were my only two choices. Sistie was tired of seeing me so pathetic and she had promised Mom and Dad that she would intervene by whatever drastic measures were necessary. I told her I would think about it. I had a mortgage obligation, a stack of unpaid bills and a very messy townhouse.

A few days later, a young man knocked at my door. He clearly had developmental challenges and difficulty speaking. I wondered if I had any cash in the house because he looked as though he might be homeless. He talked very slowly and explained that he was searching for somewhere to stay with his mama. They did not have a lot of money or a car, so they would have to live close to a store. He asked if I knew anyone in the area that might help them. Remarkably, I had no hesitation in responding. I invited him in and said, "This place is for rent."

CHAPTER TWELVE

Empowering Faith

As soon as I stepped off the plane in Sanford, Florida, I darted straight for the airport bar to celebrate. I was overjoyed to leave the Old North State behind and imagined that Orlando might be like a revolving Jurassic Park of some sort, complete with roaming alligators and ancient flying reptiles. Even the crowds of people in the terminal were an amazement because I was finally away from such a reclusive and pointless existence. There would be so many exciting sights and opportunities like Disneyworld, Epcott, and the Kennedy Space Center to explore.

When sistie picked me up, our first stop was an enchanting German restaurant downtown. I had two huge, 24 ounce mugs of beer in the glowing, warm sunshine of mid-June. It was a joyful occasion because my sister knew I could not just go cold turkey with quitting drinking, so she had a step-down plan in mind for that. Her top priority was to locate the best possible treatment for bipolar, so she literally had five full pages of providers from my insurance company. She had been making calls, reading patient reviews and researching all the prospects.

My first adjustment, however, was the massive home that my sister and brother-in-law had purchased in a prestigious neighborhood. It was impeccably decorated with antique furniture and extravagant glassware. My sister had unique talents with buying and selling collectables, so I would be living in a scaled-down version of Biltmore and it was like entering a museum for the first time. There was also an absolutely wonderful covered deck around the pool area and this quickly became my favorite sanctuary. I felt like royalty with such lavish surroundings and the back portion of the house all to myself. I also could not imagine a more inviting landscape for biking, walking and jogging. Taking up those pursuits seemed worthwhile again and the environment certainly ignited a small spark of enthusiasm in my heart.

My sister made an appointment for my intervention. I was nervous and apprehensive about the visit. What happened next commenced the beginning of prolific, permanent changes in my interpersonal world. The first, and lasting miracle, was meeting Jessica, the psychiatric P.A. who would be handling my case. She was the most beautiful, charismatic and uplifting woman I had ever encountered in my life, let alone in a mental health setting. At first, I could not believe there was a real person with this much generous devotion. Her kind, caring and attentive personality was just overwhelming and it was apparent that she had a genuine compassion for others. Her laughter and gentle reassurance were so comforting; she was someone that I trusted immediately.

Jessica was also patient in listening to our concerns, and that was something I certainly was not accustomed to. She was optimistic that I could stabilize, so I began with Lithobid, the non-generic form of lithium carbonate and the lowest dose of an anti-anxiety medication. She would keep close tabs on my progress. Sistie and I both loved her right away and could not wait for our next session with Miss Jessica.

In the meantime, the plan for slowly cutting down my alcohol consumption seemed to working, but only for about a month. I had reduced to four beers per day and started cycling and walking again for exercise. My sister wanted me to switch to light beer and continue to taper, but something in me revolted against this idea. I figured out that I could ride my bike to the convenience store and simply hide a few extra drinks in my backpack. At least, this was how the progression started again and it quickly flared into more serious infractions. Sneaking beer became too cumbersome and risky, so I decided to get airplane bottles and mix vodka or gin with Gatorade. That way, I could sit out by the pool and drink undetected. It didn't take long for my sister to notice changes in my personality.

The situation erupted in late August when I was on my way home from the store with two large cans of beer and noticed the familiar headlights of my brother-in-law's pick-up truck. He was out of town on business, so my sister's full attention was focused on my behavior. When I got into the truck, she demanded that I give her the alcohol and we began a physical struggle for control of the backpack. The battle was so fierce that the rear-view mirror was knocked down from the windshield and left dangling below the dashboard. I had been drinking liquor earlier and became easily enraged.

When we were back home, my sister issued one final warning and I ignored her request and began drinking the beer. In less than five minutes, a police officer was standing at the double doorway and cautiously walked outside. He asked me for the two cans, and I handed them both to him without incident. He then walked back inside and came out a second time to inquire if I planned on breaking things in my sister's house. I told him only the depression glassware because it was actually depressing. He stared at me intently and I let him know I was only kidding and would never destroy anything in the home. The officer told my sister that I was most likely just a "smart-ass drunk" and would probably not become violent.

I was incredibly angry at my sister in the following days, but went along with her rules regarding a couple of light beers. It was only a week before we were back in Miss Jessica's office and my sister reported the entire escapade. Sistie also stated that I was not being compliant with my bipolar medication. The ordeal was an embarrassment and I was entirely shocked when Jessica explained to me that there was no medication, no magical pill, no treatment plan and no getting better as long as I was drinking. She told me I had get involved with Alcoholics Anonymous right away because that was the only thing that would change the outcome. I absolutely did not want to even consider this course of action, and even started fabricating another method of denial whereby I could attend a few A.A. meetings and then inform Jessica that it just did not work out for me.

Then, a sense of shame and guilt came to the forefront of my mind. My sister had her head hanging down looking at her shoes and Jessica was staring at her computer screen. There was an awkward silence and I realized, even consumed with my own selfishness, that these two remarkable women were extraordinary in their efforts. They were willing to do anything to save my life. I had done nothing but lie directly to their faces and attempt to manipulate the circumstances to my benefit. I had put them both through hell for nearly four months, so why didn't they just get rid of me? Jessica could have fired me as her patient and my sister could have kicked me out of her house, but they still believed in me. They may have been disappointed or frustrated, but they were totally committed and would not surrender their faith in my restoration, even though I had continued to rack up failures.

Although it probably did not sound very convincing, I agreed to join the A.A. program. As we were leaving, Jessica smiled and I saw the very real concern and hope through her kind eyes. I admired and respected her so much that I had to at least try this new path.

I was utterly flabbergasted about how my stubborn disposition quickly dissipated when I attended my very first A.A. meeting. My sister went with me and she was also impressed. I immediately recognized all the descriptions and every story shared sounded painfully familiar. My struggles were far from unique and there was nothing different or special about my situation or even my secret, interpersonal trauma. How could these caring, gentle strangers possibly know me and fully understand my most troubling feelings? I wondered why I comprehended a new level of comfort, a kinship of encouraging support and an open forum to finally express my inner thoughts. I lost the inherent desire to rationalize, debate or even attempt to explain the connection. I did belong within this group. This was no ordinary crowd and these were my people.

Barely over a month in the program, I met Barbara. She was a most articulate, charming and devoted woman with 35 years of sobriety who became my sponsor. Actually, she followed me around after a meeting and insisted that I take her telephone number. Later, she told me I had the gift of desperation and I was a newcomer in need of direction. With her determined influence, I began working the steps and completed writing assignments per her directives. Initially, I thought I might be progressing too slowly in the program, but Barbara had to make certain that I knew the difference between willingness and willfulness. I had to let go of any notions about "my way" of thinking or doing things and understand that everything was not within my personal realm of definition.

The first three steps suggest an admission of being powerless, acceptance in a higher power and a decision to turn our lives over to the care of God as we understand him. It's important to note that God can be adopted as a working hypothesis and our understanding can be translated into positive concepts such as compassion, kindness, humility and forgiveness, for examples. The definition of a higher power could be belief in anything greater than ourselves, like the universe, the ocean or even the A.A. fellowship. As alcoholics we admit that our lives have become unmanageable and that there are no individual measures capable of restoring us.

However, would these principles assist us in coping with Covid-19 or handling any other personal challenges or crisis situations? The answer is unequivocally yes. The steps teach us to let go of control, practice patience with tolerance and develop trust that the world will slowly, but surely heal with some positive changes. These pandemics did not happen overnight and will not be resolved quickly, but we maintain faith that there will be solutions in the future that we are unaware of right now. We agree to be present in the current moment and deal with situations one day at a time.

Within the hardships and controversy around the globe, we can choose the opportunity to first invest in self-discovery and be prepared to completely alter our thoughts, actions and behaviors. We can then develop the spiritual discipline necessary to reach out to people and be of true service to others in need. Each one of us has a unique gift to share with the world, but we must identify and remove any obstacles that impair our full capabilities. A good place to start is asking for guidance about what we should be focusing on through the Serenity Prayer:

"God, grant me the serenity
To accept the things I cannot change,
The courage to change the things I can,
And the wisdom to know the difference."

In Alcoholics Anonymous, we confront our drinking and our past with full honesty and disclosure. We operate on the foundation of unity, service and recovery, while keeping sobriety as the top priority. Great sponsors in A.A, like Barbara, ask difficult questions and they are the type of inquiries necessary along the journey to understand and work the steps. We might ponder what specific things are unacceptable in our lives and why? We might want to know how acting on our own self-will has affected our life and the lives of others. We would definitely want to consider why having a closed mind is harmful to personal improvement. It would also be important to examine any issues that impact our self-esteem, self-image and self-respect.

We are beginning to look deep within ourselves and recognize what brings joy and hope into our hearts, as well. It is usually whatever can be shared with those around us. Some of us might recognize that our perception of God provides an inspiration to love. We come to realize that thinking about God's will has provided a way to heal our fractured and fragmented activities to begin focusing around a new center of reference. Now, we can experience the legitimate peace and serenity that will offer the firmness of life orientation.

Through this process, we begin to get in touch with the rhythms of a new life, which include stillness, action, listening and decision from another perspective. We learn acceptance and fulfillment while finding out who we really are and what we are really living for.

Defining a God of our comprehension offers contentment to renew ourselves through redemptive grace. So, when we are ready, we consider the third step prayer:

"God, I offer myself to Thee-
To build with me
and to do with me as Thou wilt.
Relieve me of the bondage of self,
that I may better do Thy will.
Take away my difficulties,
that victory over them may bear witness
to those I would help of Thy Power,
Thy Love, and Thy Way of life.
May I do Thy will always!"

The fourth step suggests that we complete a searching and fearless moral inventory of ourselves. This involves a tremendous amount of courage, commitment and honest determination. It is imperative that we invest substantial time and diligent effort to this process of examining everything about our entire existence. It is an extremely difficult undertaking, regardless of whether we are an alcoholic, addict or completely unaffected by any substance abuse issues. We are all human with regrets and personality traits that influence our actions, relationships and quality of life. At the very core, we have to be willing to document our resentments, fears and sexual misconduct, along with character defects and assets. We are embarking on discovering what we think, feel, sense and experience without trying to hide anything. It is important to put pen to paper with this step.

We begin with writing down a list of the people, institutions and principles that have caused us to become angry. It is important to be as specific as possible and include reasons, along with the attached emotions involved. For example, we may resent a parent, spouse or employer. We might resent a particular religion, government authority or the justice system. The same process is utilized for analyzing our particular fears that may include things like abandonment, poverty and death of a loved one. We want to consider how our resentments and fears have affected our lives and personal interactions with others.

There are detailed worksheets available online that include examples and prompt sheets to assist with these priorities. Likewise, we could utilize a worksheet to document sexual misconduct and the harm that has been done to others. This also has to be specific and must include any abusive offenses that have been committed, along with selfishness, dishonesty, bitterness, suspicion and jealousy. We should be prepared to write down where we were at fault and what should have been done instead.

We can also print off a comprehensive description of character defects and corresponding assets as a checklist. There should be at least 120 items on a valuable list to incorporate things like being prejudiced, narrow minded, manipulating or pessimistic. We want to examine what instincts, impulses or assumptions fueled our behaviors. Positive attributes might be represented by being trustworthy, fair, conscientious and altruistic. We wish to think about which assets can offset or intervene with our shortcomings.

In step five, we admit to God, to ourselves and to another human being the exact nature of our wrongs. Sharing the most intimate details of our lives will liberate us from our personal entanglements, empower our inner confidence and free our minds through total reflection. We acknowledge all our transgressions out loud, as we can truly see ourselves and our private situations as never before.

I completed my fifth step with Barbara and a member of the clergy on separate occasions. We can admit our faults to any reliable and dependable person. This individual should be someone that has proven to be responsible, respectable, confidential and safe. I immediately felt as though tremendous burdens had been lifted from me and that I would be able to move forward from a pattern of past mistakes. I discovered that I resented myself more than anyone else and was able to express those things that caused the most guilt and shame in my life. It was the beginning of my spiritual awakening because I had recognized the obstacles in my recovery and was prepared to be released from them.

In step six, we are entirely ready to have God remove all our defects of character and, in step seven, we humbly ask him to remove our shortcomings. This means that we are prepared to get rid of self-defeating, judgmental or negative attitudes and behaviors to replace them with worthwhile interactions and spiritual principles. We want to embrace the personality, temperament, mentality and disposition required for a lifelong commitment to continual improvement. It is important to also forgive ourselves and accept that love, patience and tolerance extends to ourselves, as well as others. We consider this prayer:

*"My Creator, I am now willing the You should
all of me, good and bad. I pray the You now remove
from me every single defect of character
which stands in the way of my
usefulness to You and my fellows.
Grant me strength, as I go out from here,
to do Your bidding."*

During the holiday season of 2018, I was entirely blessed to have the opportunity to write detailed letters to others in order to admit my past offenses. This was a deeply emotional experience where I was overwhelmed with the true compassion that had been so elusive to me due to my selfish obsession with alcohol. I finally realized how much I loved and cared for the people in my life through a perspective I never had before or even thought possible.

Step eight suggests that we make a list of all persons we had harmed and become willing to make amends to them. In step nine, we make direct amends to such people wherever possible, except when to do so would injure them or others. In this process, we focus on family members, friends, professional colleagues, business associates, neighbors, creditors, institutions and former enemies to dwell upon applying spiritual thought to consciously reach out to each person or specific situation.

We may make amends in person, over the telephone, through the mail or by other means as necessary. We first let go of any expectations about how our amends will be received because this process is about communicating to others that we fully recognize our faults and are regretful for our behaviors and actions. Amends may include a sincere apology, an explanation of our situation, an invitation for others to express how they feel or how they have been affected and a question about what more we might do to set things straight. This suggests more than just saying, "I'm sorry". We offer our time and share specific faults to show we are serious about efforts to repair broken bonds and heal fractured relationships. We hold ourselves accountable by admitting the things we have done and left undone, meanwhile forgiving all the wrongs done to us, (whether real or imaginary).

If someone has passed away and we cannot make direct amends, we are still responsible to make things right. We might reach out to a family member or close friend. We could honor their memory through donating or volunteering for a particular charity that was important to them. We present ourselves through someone or something else that we know they cared about. In a living amends, we create real changes through true and honest behaviors and actions. We become completely committed to a sober and healthy lifestyle for ourselves and others. In living amends, we might fulfill a promise from the past that was not kept because of addiction. We might actively improve our interactions with concerted and focused efforts. We want to be the person that our loved ones deserve by being someone who will do for them as they have done for us.

There was a positive reaction to the vast majority of the amends that I extended, and this is typically the case for most. Certain individuals may not be ready to receive amends or outright reject our most humble efforts. We may find that we gain expanded understanding or discover some relationships with others were superficial or toxic to begin with. Regardless, our higher power creates the desire to press peacefully forward with great sensitivity to the needs of others so that we can offer unique expressions and praise to those we have wronged. We contemplate, through prayer and meditation, the correct time and method for our amends.

Although A.A. is a spiritual program and is not aligned with any particular religion, it is certainly acceptable to utilize additional sources of inspiration (outside of meetings) for personal guidance. In my case, there was a particular Bible verse that was extremely helpful and relevant to these steps.

"So, chosen by God for this new life of love,
dress in the wardrobe God picked out for you:
compassion, kindness, humility,
quiet strength, discipline. Be even-tempered,
content with second place, quick
to forgive any offense. Forgive as quickly and
completely as God forgave you. And
regardless of what else you put on, wear love.
It's your basic, all-purpose garment.
Never be without it."
Colossians 3:12-14

Although still early on in my sobriety, I felt a sense of peace and spiritual tranquility that was completely transforming me. I certainly could not take much individual credit because I was surrounded and supported by so many giving individuals.

Barbara was absolutely tireless in her sponsorship efforts. We attended two meetings a week together, where I also completed service work through preparing coffee and refreshments. In addition, we spoke by telephone every single day and met privately once or twice per week. Her direction was imperative to my success and understanding. She reminded me constantly that the role of alcohol was literally a matter of life or death. If I complained or edged near a pity-party of any sort, she would intervene to ask me what my part was in the situation. She explained to me that I could no longer use mental illness as a crutch or an excuse.

Barbara led by example, practicing the principles in all her affairs. She challenged me to be fearless, examine all my motives and then move forward with renewed determination. My sobriety had to be the top priority, along with staying close to the fellowship. I had to learn to accept life on life's terms and understand that there was literally nothing that alcohol would not make worse.

Jessica was also a devoted and consistent advocate for my recovery. She stabilized all my medications, to include Vraylar, which is a newer, atypical antipsychotic that also treats depression. It is an expensive alternative, so she made sure that I always had an abundance of samples from her office.

Although Jessica's role could have been limited to prescriptions and monitoring my medications, she inspired me in ways that I would not imagine possible. Even as I struggled in developing a new sense of identity and purpose, she went out of her way to express a sincere belief in my abilities to overcome any obstacles. It was though she was willing to hold my hand through the deepest, darkest waters of self-doubt and constantly reassure me that I was not going to drown.

I had encouragement from many, but Jessica's influence was different because she always knew instinctively exactly what to say or write. In my stark hours of depression, she would respond with an uplifting email and I would be reminded how blessed I was that this incredible woman was my biggest cheerleader. She truly believed in my potential on a higher level than anyone else. She awakened in me a sense of untapped accountability for an important destiny. It was not a contemplation of existence I would have ever reached without her influence. I never imagined that I might go on to actually help others, but I certainly knew that I wished to be more like Jessica.

I wondered how she extended such enthusiasm, hope and comfort to so many. It certainly was not within her job description to go out on a limb for me or anyone else, yet she exhibited the qualities that one could only expect to encounter in a guardian angel. I could have been just another mentally ill patient with substance abuse issues, but I never, ever felt that way. In fact, I knew she was an honest, forthcoming person. Her elevated opinion about me meant a world of difference in my motivation to advance in the program and become the best possible version of myself. Jessica steered me away from the limits of labeling myself a bipolar alcoholic. Those were diseases that did not have to define my personality or dictate my future.

No one ever says, "I am cancer," or "I am Multiple Sclerosis," or "I am Alzheimer's." It is imperative that bipolar is something that I deal with and not something that I am. I do say that I am alcoholic because that is part of the program of unity and humility. It is also a tradition of togetherness that places us all within in the same, equal status for singleness of purpose with reaching out to other alcoholics.

Interpersonally, I was finally accepting the positive reinforcements and believing in the changes. I was beginning a life-altering journey with a renewed sense of direction that there were greater things on the horizon.

CHAPTER THIRTEEN

Gratitude Shines

My level of progress and resolve was tested very early on in the A.A. program. In fact, I only had six months of sobriety and had yet to complete the final steps. Closeness within the fellowship and appointments with Jessica always served to rejuvenate my energies, but I was still somewhat in a mental fog and was tired a lot of the time. Routine blood work revealed that I was in iron overload and I was referred to a hematologist. It was discovered that I had genetic mutations for a disorder known as hereditary hemochromatosis, which means the body absorbs and stores too much iron. This condition has to be monitored because it can cause damage to major organs. In my case, the suggestion was a modified diet and donating blood. Of greater concern was my gastrointestinal system, given my history of pancreatitis. It would seem prudent to visit a digestive specialist and that is what I did, where several diagnostic tests were performed.

My sister and I had attended a follow-up appointment together with the gastroenterologist after I received an MRI scan of my complete abdominal area. I still had discomfort in my pancreas region and was feeling frequently exhausted. When the doctor came into the patient room, he glanced at the computer screen briefly and clicked through several images.

He then informed me that I had stage 4 cirrhosis of the liver. He did not even look up at me. He was very casual in reporting that the damage was extensive and I would need to consider going on a waiting list for a transplant.

My sister and I were completely taken off guard and I actually went into some sort of shock-like state, while struggling to think of questions to ask. I wondered if it could be reversed or my liver might heal itself, but this doctor offered no chance for these possibilities. He said it was good that I had stopped drinking, handed me a brochure about a liver transplant, and left the room. I was utterly devastated. I had just been handed a death sentence and I knew it. However, I had no reason to doubt the prognosis. I had wasted over 30 years drinking heavily and now I was presented with the physical consequences.

I immediately did all the possible Internet research and discovered that 50% of those with alcoholic cirrhosis survive two years and only 35% make it five years. I also learned that I could expect worsening symptoms and complications to include fluid buildup, internal bleeding and frequent bouts of nausea with vomiting. There would be a mental deterioration to include confusion, disorientation and difficulty concentrating. In addition, I would have to prove additional months of sobriety before registration for a liver transplant.

Given the severity level of my case and the waiting list, it was much more probable that I would die before the possibility of a transplant. I retrieved all this information within the first 24 hours of my diagnosis. It did not take me long to comprehend the reality of the situation and I just began to pray. I did not ask God for any instant healing or divine intervention because I had learned a new way to communicate with my higher power. Everything was not about me and my self-centered expectations. I only wanted dignity, endurance and the strength of acceptance. My prayers were quickly answered, and I could sense the emotional shift in my mindset.

Although I was extremely depressed inwardly, I was surprised by my positive attitude and determined faith. I only shared the news with a handful of those closest to me and Barbara was impressed that I seemed calm, upbeat and encouraging. Mom absolutely did not believe the news. She remarked that my uncle had lived many years with cirrhosis, but I thought she was, quiet understandably, in denial about me. She was insistent that I did not have this liver disease and was adamant that I get a second opinion. It was a mother's intuition and she did always have a sixth sense about certain things.

I had grown so much spiritually that I was willing to accept whatever God's will was for my life without question. My only concern was for the people who loved me. I did not want to worry them or be a burden as my illness progressed. Most of all, I did not want them to be upset if God chose to call me home early. I was not afraid of death at all and thought maybe I could assist other alcoholics by sharing my story while I was still able to do so. This was a level of understanding for divine grace and purpose in my life that I had never experienced before. I was most grateful that the program and the steps had prepared me to respond to the ultimate challenge. I marveled at how this news actually increased my care and concern for others. I wanted my family and friends to be at peace with the diagnosis, so I began practicing how I could help them cope with the situation.

I also had a revelation during this period of adjustment. I finally understood why dearest Bobby listed my telephone number as the first contact following his death. It was a warning to me. It was a foreboding message that I did not heed. He was my best friend and we were so much alike. Even our birthdays were just days apart. He knew I was on the exact same course of disaster and he tried to get through to me about my own demise. There would be no special considerations just because we both endured bipolar. He saw that I was headed down the precise path he had taken with alcohol. Bobby was trying to tell me that drinking would ruin my life and then kill me, just like it took him at the early age of 58. Now I understood, but it was too late. Still, I could refuse to crumble psychologically and be an example of courage. I could offer the warnings to others for as long as possible. It was also important to me that I get through all of the steps myself and now there was a call of urgency.

It was nearly a week after the dreaded prognosis when the miracle happened. Actually, it was a shocking revelation, but a miracle nonetheless. My sister, in her own state of disbelief and suspicion, went down to the imaging center to get a disc copy and written report of my MRI. I signed the consent forms, but did not want her to get the information. I thought it would just be adding misery to read the gory details and look at pictures of how alcohol had destroyed my now diseased liver.

Then, she called me on her cell phone and she was screaming. I could not understand one word she was saying. I know she was cursing some, but I could not tell if she was overjoyed or enraged. Actually, she was both at the same time. Finally, she settled down enough to tell me that my entire report was basically a clean bill of health. Specifically, it was documented that my liver was normal and there were no signs of cirrhosis. I still did not believe it. I wanted to see that paper right in front of me and then call someone to verify that it was really my situation. I did not know what to think. I did not know what to do or how to react. How could a horrendous mistake of this magnitude even be possible?

I wanted to be angry like my sister, but I just did not have it in me in that very moment. I was too grateful that I was going to live. I had just experienced five of the longest days in self-reflection and extended prayer of my entire life. It never occurred to me that my medical records could have been mixed up with another patient. That is not something that happens with modern technology and triple-checking identifications for procedures. How in the world could a doctor be so careless and confused, especially with a serious, life-threatening diagnosis? These may have been questions initially flashing through my mind, but they were quickly replaced with peaceful thoughts. I realized God had answered my prayers about how to go forward, but he also responded to the prayers of my immediate family and closest friends. They must have asked that it be a mistake or that it wasn't true or that I misunderstood or even that it completely disappear. I know that was my Mom's prayer.

My sister and I did go back to confront the doctor and he admitted to nothing. He said he wanted a liver biopsy and my sister and I were both confused about medical coding. He made very little sense in his explanations, but we knew the truth. I was so thankful that my sister was present as a witness for the previous appointment. Perhaps, this doctor was concerned about legal ramifications and I did not expect an apology from him. This was a learning process for me and cirrhosis could have easily been the real outcome because I had abused my body for so long with alcohol. The entire ordeal happened for a reason and served to test my faith and increase my spiritual awareness, so I could not wait to contact the people I loved to let them know that I was going to be around for a while longer.

My endearment for my sister had also finally reached a new level of comprehension. Poor sistie had always been there to save me or intervene or negotiate on my behalf. I knew she did not get enough credit for her efforts and I had often taken her for granted. She had been trying to protect me since high school and would sacrifice anything for my health and happiness.

There were times that I thought she was too controlling or overbearing, but her tenacity was always to represent my best interests. Most siblings would have never invested themselves or committed the care and tireless assistance that she had given to me.

Sistie represented herself in a leadership role for the entire extended family. She was the first point of contact for anyone in need and that was due to her quick resolve in finding solutions. Although she had raised three children while she was very young and now had five adoring grandchildren, her connection to me was entirely special. She was the only one to pull me out of the gutter when I hit rock bottom, so she facilitated the path to saving my life. There was no way to thank her or adequately show my appreciation. I could only wish that she could see the changes in me and recognize that she initiated the process. In a single incidence, she once said to me, "You are my one and only sister and I am not going to lose you no matter what it takes." She has certainly been a true champion for me and always kept her word.

Following the medical incident, I was ever more committed to progress through the program. Ten, Eleven and Twelve are maintenance steps where we devote ourselves to ongoing spiritual growth. Step ten suggests that we continue to take personal inventory and when we are wrong, promptly admit it. This basically means that we have swept our side of the street clean from the past, and we can now pick up the leaves on a daily basis. We have developed an abundance of inward courage and outward confidence in acknowledging our shortcomings and taking charge of our actions. We have also learned to pay attention to how our behaviors and reactions affect others. Whenever the outcome is negative or harmful, we immediately take responsibility and move forward to repair any damage.

At the end of every day, we ask ourselves if we have been resentful, selfish or dishonest. Is there anyone that we owe an apology to? Is there something that we should discuss with someone else right away? Is there anything that we could have done better for ourselves or others? We strive to stay in tune with our new, positive outlook and recognize any problems long before they take hold.

Likewise, Step eleven states that we sought through prayer and meditation to improve our conscious contact with God <u>as we understood Him</u>, praying only for knowledge of His will for us and the power to carry that out. We want to approach all activities in joyful awareness of God's presence, so we humbly ask for his will regarding any frustrations or concerns. As we practice devotion, we find ourselves going through the stresses and strains of any challenges with an ease and serenity that amazes us. We have learned to trust prayer and meditation to provide wisdom and knowledge in approaching each new situation. Like so many other disciplines, we actually commit time in it so that more may be revealed to us to elevate our thinking. Our faith has now become a conscious experience that revives patience and tolerance in our actions for ourselves and others. Through this step, we walk without fear and full of hope and strength to do God's will. We live prayfully so that we are constantly ready to receive the directives that expand and renew us. We know that prayer and meditation calms us down and grounds us, usually helping to alleviate any worries that might threaten our recovery. We go forward with the ability to share compassion for ourselves and others, so we consider this prayer:

Lord, make me an instrument of thy peace.
That where there is hatred, I may bring love.
That where there is wrong, I may bring
the spirit of forgiveness.
That where there is discord, I may bring harmony.
That where there is error, I may bring truth.
That where there is doubt, I may bring faith.
That where there is despair, I may bring hope.
That where there are shadows, I may bring light.
That where there is sadness, I may bring joy.
Lord, grant that I may seek rather to comfort,
than to be comforted.
To understand, than to be understood.
To love, than to be loved.
For it is by self-forgetting that one finds.
It is by forgiving that one is forgiven.
It is by dying that one awakens to Eternal Life.
—Saint Francis of Assisi—

We have learned through the steps how to be content with slow development and grow in grace in spite of any challenges. We go through all our daily activities in joyful awareness of God's presence and a willingness to share the prayers of gratitude that flow from our hearts. In this process, we have also developed a new level of understanding about the outer burdens and inward uneasiness that exists in others.

Our reflective way of living has heightened our senses to all those still suffering and we now have the unique capacity to illuminate change. We help give focus to others along their journey of recovery or encouragement in whatever hardship another is enduring. From the book, *Twelve Steps and Twelve Traditions*, "we will also report that out of every season of grief or suffering, when the hand of God seemed heavy or even unjust, new lessons for living were learned and new resources of courage were uncovered."

Step twelve states that having had a spiritual awakening as a result of these steps, we tried to carry the message to alcoholics, and to practice these principles in all our affairs. We have been able to persevere and resolve the past so that we are prepared for clarity and action in any situation. Trusting a higher power, cleaning house, sharing our experiences and becoming involved in community or service work creates a living example of caring devotion to progress.

We are now in possession of honesty, tolerance, peace of mind and unconditional love. The steps have placed in our hands a wonderful key that we can utilize to unlock the doors and assist in setting others free. Sometimes extending hope is just ensuring that we are warm, caring and non-judgmental in our approach.

In completing the steps, the *Big Book* of Alcoholics Anonymous states that we have "recovered from a seemingly hopeless state of mind and body." However, it also says "we are not cured of alcoholism. What we really have is a daily reprieve contingent on the maintenance of our spiritual condition." Therefore, we take one day at a time in all our contemplations, remaining close to our higher power for inspiration.

Within step twelve, we discover genuine purpose and direction. We learn that true ambition is the deep desire to live usefully and walk with grace. It is also interesting to note that we have a guideline for the perimeters of self-importance and a method to determine appropriate leadership. In these unprecedented troubling events in our nation and around the world, we can better understand our role and determine the influence of others. For example, the *Twelve and Twelve* states: "When by devoted service to family, friends, business or community, we attract wide-spread affection and are sometimes singled out for posts of greater responsibility and trust, we try to be humbly grateful and exert ourselves the more in a spirit of love and service. True leadership, we find, depends upon an example and not upon vain displays of power or glory."

I take the approach of always rekindling my relationship with God for growth and redemption. I am gracefully broken, but gratefully restored in order to share my story with others just beginning or rejoining their journey of recovery. This is why sponsorship is such a cherished responsibility. I must have continuous commitment on an individual basis to other alcoholics attempting to attain or maintain sobriety through A.A. The shortest definition just means two alcoholics working together to put the program into action. However, an insightful sponsor devotes a substantial amount of time and energy into the healing process for others. That type of role is more like a mentorship to teach the steps, answer questions, provide support and extend guidance on a consistent basis.

Having the right sponsor is critical to success and both have to be willing to form a caring partnership. It is not uncommon for a sponsor and sponcee to be together for many, many years and most form life-long friendships.

It is extremely important to note that A.A. has a singleness of purpose to carry the message to the alcoholic who still suffers. Back in the 1950's, there were those that predicted that A.A. could well become a new spearhead for a spiritual awakening throughout the world. The founders made it clear that it would be misleading to give the impression that A.A. solves other problems. Experience with alcohol is one thing that all A.A. members have in common. Each group prudently represents this primary purpose and all meeting topics revolve around the issue of alcohol.

It is also imperative to understand that the concept of a higher power in A.A. does not require any particular system of belief or religion. There are all women or all men meetings, Atheist/Agnostic meetings and specialized groups for LGBTQ participants. The primary message of recovery from alcoholism remains the same across all groups, although the format might slightly vary. A.A. has a spiritual foundation and the only requirement is a desire to stop drinking. This is indicated in a portion of the preamble that states: "A.A. is not allied with any sect, denomination, politics, organization or institution; does not wish to engage in any controversy; neither endorses nor opposes any causes." As per the traditions of A.A., Alcoholics Anonymous has no opinion on outside issues, and anonymity provides protection and privacy to other members. Likewise, what is shared in meetings is confidential. However, A.A. is not a secret society and is not invisible.

CHAPTER FOURTEEN

Transforming Destiny

When Covid-19 paralyzed activities across the globe, Alcoholics Anonymous responded swiftly and decisively to keep the program operational. In fact, there were 24/7 Zoom meetings and groups everywhere made the transition in the most expedient fashion. This actually created new opportunities for members to log into Zoom and participate anywhere in the world. Since alcohol abuse was skyrocketing, newcomers were involving themselves in record numbers. This was also the case for online support groups and A.A. chat rooms. It is a blessing that so many are benefitting from the step work. Those unfamiliar with the program are learning how the twelve steps influence every aspect of their lives. It is also true that those already grounded in the foundation of the steps are better prepared to deal with Covid-19 and the associated challenges.

As demonstrated by *Twelve Steps and Twelve Traditions*, step work teaches us to handle the outcome of any situation. The book poses several questions: "How shall we come to terms with seeming failure or success? Can we now accept and adjust to either without despair or pride? Can we accept poverty, sickness, loneliness and bereavement with courage and serenity? Can we steadfastly content ourselves with the humbler, yet sometimes more durable, satisfactions when the brighter, more glittering achievements are denied us? The A.A. answer to these questions in yes, all these things are possible. We know this because we see monotony, pain and even calamity turned to good use by those who keep on trying to practice the twelve steps. And if these are the facts of life for the many alcoholics who have recovered, they can become the facts of life for many more."

The actual twelve steps themselves represent a massive untapped resource in dealing with the social and interpersonal demands presented by Covid-19. The solution to most problems resides in our own attitudes, mindsets and level of spiritual awareness. Even when everything is going wrong, there is a deeper, more long-term perspective that we can take to see the potential good in any situation. The key to maintaining our own emotional well-being is to encourage and comfort others. Psychology Today states that the wisdom of Twelve Step programs will assist any one with navigating Covid-19 because when we reach out in compassion and understanding, we are helping ourselves get better too. The article states that, "Research on heroism tells us that we are all designed to do what classic heroes do, encounter adversity, seek help from friends, make mental adjustments, behave accordingly, and then share our experience, strength and hope with others. The hero's journey is the 12-step journey."

During these pandemics, there will continue to be social and political unrest, along with economic disparity, stressful environments and different ways of doing things. However, not all of the modifications have been negative. People are accessing more educational resources online for their kids; finding unconventional ways to connect with coworkers, friends, and family; and employers are being more flexible in how they respond to employee needs through advanced, dynamic technology. We have also seen the largest work-from-home experiment ever conducted in human history, so some of these factors will likely become permanent fixtures.

In fact, business and corporate leaders could also benefit from the 12-step model because it is one the most successful change management programs ever developed. Many companies are now re-evaluating and restructuring, so the steps could create a professional atmosphere that is honest, collaborative, supportive and cohesive. Raising the level of self-awareness through character building and personnel development would assist work teams with their problem solving skills and help construct a culture of respect. Outside consultants could be utilized for strategy and implementation for individual businesses, while still keeping the integrity of each step.

On an interpersonal level, our lives move onward with all types of obstacles, so now is the time for us to engage in practices to become the very best versions of ourselves. It is a responsibility for each of us to consider improving and transforming so that we represent true courage in crisis. This means that we are prepared to respond to any circumstance with faith, patience and tolerance. We have to be willing to open our hearts and our minds because people need us now more than ever. Some of us will be called upon to take personal or professional roles that we never considered. Some of us will have to modify plans that we have been creating for a lifetime. Some of us will have to make sacrifices that we never would have anticipated. Each of us has suffered in unique ways and our support is invaluable to someone else facing a similar situation, so we create the new avenues of generosity that are desperately necessary.

One of the co-founders of A.A., Bill W., wrote about how critical it is to embrace transition. He said, "Let us never fear needed change. Certainly we have to discriminate between changes for worse and changes for better. But once a need becomes clearly apparent in an individual, in a group, or in A.A. as a whole, it has long since been found out that we cannot stand still and look the other way. The essence of all growth is a willingness to change for the better and then an unremitting willingness to shoulder whatever responsibility this entails."

In these times, it is important to stop and remind ourselves of the power of our own resilience and flexibility. We have all been challenged before, and we can gain perspective and determination from those experiences by recalling how we coped, and then applying that knowledge to the present moment. Those practicing the 12 steps already have a mindset for acceptance and perseverance.

While being enormously disruptive and traumatic, the crisis can also nurture the emergence of great common purpose, solidarity, creativity and improvisation. These are the type of characteristics that can also be further inspired through the 12-steps. Organizations and anonymous groups around the globe have been utilizing the steps for decades to address narcotics, gambling, overeating and sex addiction, just to name a few. There are also programs for workaholics and those with hoarding problems. The steps have been successfully addressing addiction for 85 years and can certainly provide the blueprint for restoration in this troublesome era. In addition, we can revisit any of the steps at any time. As our personal or professional lives modify, then we go back to the steps most relevant to provide guidance.

Following step nine, where we make our amends to others, there is a specific list of promises to further motivate our efforts and demonstrate what we can expect to experience.

These include the following:

- *We are going to know a new freedom and a new happiness.*
- *We will not regret the past, nor wish to shut the door on it.*
- *We will comprehend the word serenity.*
- *We will know peace.*
- *No matter how far down the scale we have gone, we will see how our experience can benefit others.*
- *That feeling of uselessness and self-pity will disappear.*
- *We will lose interest in selfish things and gain insight into our fellows.*
- *Self-seeking will slip away.*
- *Our whole attitude and outlook will change.*
- *Fear of people and economic insecurity will leave us.*
- *We will intuitively know how to handle situations which used to baffle us.*
- *We will suddenly realize that God is doing for us what we could not do for ourselves.*

These are not extravagant promises. I have already realized many of them myself, even in early sobriety. While everyone has a unique spiritual journey, there are countless stories and testimonials from others who have abundantly recognized these transitions. Again, the promises are available to anyone willing to work the 12-steps.

Meanwhile, all the long-term influences of Covid-19 may be unknown, but most experts agree that it is not going away anytime soon. It is possible that this current outbreak will be followed by a massive second wave that is twice as large and long-lasting. This is exactly what happened with the 1918 Spanish flu pandemic; a moderate wave in March 1918 was followed by an explosion in cases that September, followed by smaller peaks until early 1919. Unless a vaccine is developed soon, there could be Covid-19 outbreaks through the end of 2022, until at least half of the world has been infected. However, the World Health Organization believes a vaccine global access facility could stop the acute phase in 2021 through reaching the most vulnerable 20% of the population in participating countries. The goal is to gain control, as the virus may never be totally eradicated.

The United States government is ordering potential vaccines directly, which would be free or affordable for Americans. It is possible that the U.S. could end up with a vaccine that, on average, only reduces a person's risk of a Covid-19 infection by just 50%. This would be about equal to the effective rate of vaccines for influenza, according to the CDC. Although scientists are hoping for a higher percentage, medical experts emphasize that the public health approach must never be abandoned.

There will still be a problem if large numbers of people refuse to be vaccinated, similar to parents who do not inoculate their children against measles. The next battle on the horizon could be for states to require Covid-19 vaccinations for certain segments of the population or legislate compliance to get a passport, utilize public transportation or go to a gym. In the future, private employers and colleges will also have to decide whether or not to require students and staff to be vaccinated. Beyond mandates, public education campaigns can be utilized with trusted community members, religious leaders and celebrities.

There were repeated warnings from public health officials about safety protocols over the summer as coronavirus cases continued to surge and intensive care unit beds were reaching capacity in certain areas. Although there is increased testing, younger patients in Florida represented cases linked to bars and parties. The states that reopened early saw the biggest increases. According to the Washington Post, top federal health officials predict that infections could worsen in many states without new restrictions.

In addition, for those still suggesting herd immunity through infections, Dr. Anthony Fauci, the top U.S. infectious disease expert, noted that with the number of people with diabetes and obesity in America, "the death toll would be enormous and totally unacceptable." Herd immunity includes the idea that a sufficient number of people will eventually develop antibodies to stop the virus spread. The Swedish government tried this method, as Covid-19 overwhelmed many European nations. Sweden failed to implement any strict lockdown procedures and opted for voluntary measures. As a result, public health officials noted the strategy led to death, grief and suffering. Allowing an infection rate in the U.S. of 65% to 70% of the population would translate into a morally reprehensible toll of more than one million deaths, according to Cornell University immunology researchers. Moreover, it is still early on in the pandemic and a positive result on an antibody test would not guarantee immunity.

Due mostly to inconsistent messages, conflicting reports and misinformation, there are those still doubting the validity and seriousness of the coronavirus. Some anti-mask protestors say their rights are being violated, while others do not trust the sources of scientific evidence. The fact that wearing a mask provoked some violent reactions is disappointing, especially if a person's notion of perceived freedom is to behave exactly as he or she wishes, regardless of the consequences to others. Although these behaviors could be categorized as inconsiderate, selfish, irrational, stubborn or uninformed, it is best to remember that no one likes to be judged, criticized or embarrassed. The rules have also been different from place to place, and this has added to confusion and frustration. If mandates are implemented across the board, then compliance would increase, similar to regulations for wearing seat belts.

Many of us are aware that facts, science and justice are not conspiracies, nor should they be defined by divisive partisan politics. Americans have been called upon to absorb a lot of trauma in a short period of time and some have felt threatened, while others have revolted from fear of the unknown. Approaching conflict resolution with angry participants, regardless of the issues, seldom produces any productive results. Therefore, we have to invest in unity, search for common bonds, become willing to admit our shortcomings, transform into active listeners and develop tolerant attitudes. This process has to start at the individual level.

The *Big Book of A.A.* suggests that if are "willing" to accept our mistakes, poor choices and experiences, we can begin learning development. Everything we are exposed to in life presents us with another valuable lesson the very second that we take responsibility for our own actions. As controversy surrounds every aspect of our existence, we do not want to remain in denial, while constantly placing blame elsewhere. Therefore, we have to commit to allowing ourselves to observe behaviors (our own and those of others) from an objective standpoint. This requires a devotion to self-examination and an openness to new or different ideas. As the 18th century British theologian William Paley, presented: "There is a principle which is a bar against all information, which is proof against all arguments and which cannot fail to keep a man in everlasting ignorance – that principle is contempt prior to investigation." There has been a theme in current events of making conclusions before having all the facts and this trend will always hamper progress for the greater good.

As step twelve suggests, we can accept accountability to carry a positive message to others without expectations through setting uplifting examples. Our own cheerfulness, energy level and satisfaction with overall life can be demonstrated through personal attitudes. Researchers suspect that positivity protects against the damage of stress and helps us to make better decisions by focusing more on long-term goals. Studies also find that negative emotions can weaken our immune system response, so it is imperative to develop habits that improve the future outlook. Behavioral experts at John Hopkins have found that we can advance happier outcomes across a spectrum of conditions through things like humor therapy, reframing our thoughts and building resiliency. The ability to adapt with the situations and losses from Covid-19 can be augmented by maintaining closer relationships and accepting that change is a part of life. Most importantly, we must take action on problems rather than hoping they disappear or waiting for them to resolve themselves.

As former first lady Michelle Obama suggests, we are mustering up unimaginable courage. Even when it feels so overwhelming, we must work so that all of us can keep moving forward for justice and progress. She states: "This is who we still are: compassionate, resilient, decent people whose fortunes are bound up with one another. And it is well past time for our leaders to once again reflect our truth. So, it is up to us to add our voices and our votes to the course of history, echoing heroes like John Lewis who said, "When you see something that is not right, you must say something. You must do something." That is the truest form of empathy: not just feeling, but doing; not just for ourselves or our kids, but for everyone, for all our kids."

Surely, we can agree that our relationships, interactions and daily living or work routines are in a state of evolvement as never before. We will have to transition to new norms, rearrange our environment and respond to continual modifications whether we are prepared or not. We have to deal with the psychological distress now because that is the single greatest factor in how we process and respond to challenges. Currently, there can be post-traumatic growth where we actually discover inner strength (our character assets) and a deeper sense of gratitude. This will allow us to approach the right priorities in our life with humble grace, while learning to stay in a place of understanding.

The other co-founder of A.A., Dr. Bob, kept a plaque on his desk that read, "Humility is perpetual quietness of the heart. It is to have no trouble. It is never to be fretted, or vexed, irritable or sore; to wonder at nothing that is done to me, to feel nothing against me. It is to be at rest when nobody praises me, and when I am blamed or despised, it is to have a blessed home in myself where I can go in and shut the door and kneel to my Father in secret and be at peace, as in a deep sea of calmness, when all around and about is seeming trouble."

Certainly, our vulnerability has been exposed and our weaknesses may have become magnified. However, we can create new beginnings, extend offers of support to others and raise the level of awareness about the ongoing social, political and economic dilemmas that disrupt our lives. This means acknowledging that there is always someone in greater need than we are and that there are always people in similar circumstances facing the exact same struggles that we are enduring. In addition, we have to be diligent in observing our environment to become more pro-active in reaching out because not everyone is able or willing to ask for help.

When Senator Kamala Harris first accepted the nomination to become Vice President of the United States, she immediately acknowledged that we are a nation in grieving from the losses created by the coronavirus. She called attention to the inequities and injustice that have caused Black, Latino and Indigenous people to suffer and die disproportionately. She stated: "This virus has no eyes, and yet it knows exactly how we see each other—and how we treat each other. And let's be clear—there is no vaccine for racism. We've got to do the work. For George Floyd. For Breonna Taylor. For the lives of too many others to name. For our children. For all of us. We've got to do the work to fulfill that promise of equal justice under law. Because, none of us are free...until all of us are free...We're at an inflection point. The constant chaos leaves us adrift. The incompetence makes us feel afraid. The callousness makes us feel alone. It's a lot. And here's the thing: We can do better and deserve so much more"

There are ongoing decisions to be made at the local, state and national levels that will impact everyone. Our individual participation is critical in the determination of how the future landscape will look for our children, families and communities. Non-profit prevention initiatives especially need our support and volunteer efforts as they adjust to improve trust and inclusiveness in program services for at-risk clients. We have the unprecedented opportunity to be more informed, vocal and accountable for creating many empowering alternatives. Our personal adaptation will make a difference in how we respond and in how we grow with change.

As *the Twelve and Twelve* explains, "For the wise have always known that no one can make much of his life until self-searching becomes a regular habit, until he is able to admit and accept what he finds, and until he patiently and persistently tries to correct what is wrong."

The dire predictions about increased substance abuse and additional mental health problems do not need to become realities. We have had the right answers before our eyes since 1935 in the twelve steps. Likewise, we can come together in restored dignity and resolve to fight these pandemics in a unified fashion with faith in the core values of our democracy. We can move beyond the chaos, divisiveness and speculation to place honesty above hysteria. We can put progress above panic and principles before personalities. we have to open our hearts and our minds while offering our unique contributions as though this nation and world depends upon each of us, because it does.

Let our legacy be one that promotes empathy, compromise and understanding, so that when our children, grandchildren and great-grandchildren ask how we survived, they will be utterly shocked by the stories of our generous efforts. We will be able to tell them that we responded with genuine compassion for those who needed it the most, when they needed it the most. We will share why we put our disagreements aside to help our fellow Americans suffering from sickness, poverty, inequality, discrimination, victimization and limited resources. Future generations will know that we took a stand and made a difference in the most vulnerable lives.

When this country was at the crossroads of disaster, we showed up for our desperate citizens. We gave whatever was necessary. We sacrificed wherever we could. We became involved in charity and outreach programs as never before because people needed us and it was the right thing to do. We may have started out struggling by ourselves and stabilizing our own environment, but then realized we had a higher destiny. We answered the call for help. In becoming the best version of ourselves, we saved the lives of others. And that is how we want to be remembered.

There can be a spiritual revolution across the globe. It can happen one person at a time, one step at a time and one day at a time.

Through our sincere endeavors, we will finally be able to do, feel and believe that which we could not accomplish (or even imagine) before. So, we should not be surprised when the things we never dared to dream begin to spring into joyful reality. The most heartfelt longings for our lives can become true through new courage in adversity. This gift, which is a higher state of consciousness and being, is why we keep what we have by giving it away. In simple terms, when we work for the best interests of others, our own lives continue to improve and evolve for the better.

Bibliography

Ad Fontes Media, "Media Bias Chart," July 19, 2020, available at https://www.adfontesmedia.com/.

Allison, Scott, T., "How the Wisdom of 12-Step Programs can Help Us with Covid-19," Psychology Today, March 30, 2020, available at https://www.psychologytoday.com/us/blog/why-we-need-heroes/202003/how-the-wisdom-12-step-programs-can-help-us-covid-19.

American Addiction Center, "Alcohol and Drug Abuse Statistics," June 1, 2020, available at https://americanaddictioncenters.org/rehab-guide/addiction-statistics.

Anti-Defamation League, "Deadly Shooting at the Tree of Life Synagogue," available at https://www.adl.org/education/educator-resources/lesson-plans/deadly-shooting-at-the-tree-of-life-synagogue.

Anti-Defamation League, "Our History: In the 1910's," available at https://www.adl.org/who-we-are/history#in-the-1910s.

Azarian, Bobby, "A complete Psychological Analysis of Trump's Support," Psychology Today, December 27, 2018, available at https://www.psychologytoday.com/us/blog/mind-in-the-machine/201812/complete-psychological-analysis-trumps-support.

Banks D, Couzens L, Planty M., "Assessment of coverage in the arrest-related deaths program," U.S. Department of Justice, 2015. Available at: https://www.bjs.gov/content/pub/pdf/acardp.pdf.

BBC News, "Coronavirus: The Queen's Message Seen by 24 Million," April 6, 2020, available at https://www.bbc.com/news/entertainment-arts-52183327.

Cillizza, Chris., "How 2 Ex-Presidents Showed What Real Leadership Looks Like," The Point, CNN, May 8, 2020, available at https://www.cnn.com/2020/05/08/politics/barack-obama-george-w-bush-coronavirus-leadership/index.html.

Clark, Simon., "How White Supremacy Returned to Mainstream Politics," Center for American Progress, July 1, 2020, available at https://www.americanprogress.org/issues/security/reports/2020/07/01/482414/white-supremacy-returned-mainstream-politics/.

CNN Politics, "Transcript: Kamala Harris' DNC Speech," August 20, 2020, available at https://www.cnn.com/2020/08/19/politics/kamala-harris-speech-transcript/index.html

CNN Politics, "Transcript: Michelle Obama's DNC Speech," August 18, 2020, available at https://www.cnn.com/2020/08/17/politics/michelle-obama-speech-transcript/index.html

Dewan, Shaila., Kovaleski, Serge, F., "Thousands of Complaints do Little to Change Police Ways," *The New York Times*, June 8, 2020, available at https://www.nytimes.com/2020/05/30/us/derek-chauvin-george-floyd.html.

Fausset, R., Rojas, R., "John Lewis, A Man of Unbreakable Perseverance is Laid to Rest.", *The New York Times*, July 30, 2020, available at https://www.nytimes.com/2020/07/30/us/john-lewis-live-funeral.html.

Garret, L., Moore, J. "Herd Immunity Works – If you don't care how many people die," *Fortune, July 27, 2020, available at* https://fortune.com/2020/07/27/herd-immunity-coronavirus-covid-sweden/.

Gateway Foundation, "Deaths of Despair during the Coronavirus," May 26, 2020 available at https://www.gatewayfoundation.org/addiction-blog/coronavirus-deaths-of-despair/.

Global Initiative Against Transnational Organized Crime, "Aggravating Circumstances: How Coronavirus Impacts Human Trafficking," June 2, 2020, Available at https://globalinitiative.net/human-trafficking-covid-impact/.

Hayden, Michael Edison., "Stephen Miller's Affinity for White Nationalism Revealed in Leaked Emails," Southern Poverty Law Center, November 12, 2019, available at https://www.splcenter.org/hatewatch/2019/11/12/stephen-millers-affinity-white-nationalism-revealed-leaked-emails.

HIV Vaccines, "Potential Future Options," HIV.gov, June 16, 2020, available at https://www.hiv.gov/hiv-basics/hiv-prevention/potential-future-options/hiv-vaccines.

Hoffman, Jan.,"With Meetings Banned, Millions Struggle to Stay Sober on Their Own," *The New York Times*, March 26, 2020, available at https://www.nytimes.com/2020/03/26/health/coronavirus-alcoholics-drugs-online.html.

Holland, Kimberly., "What Covid-19 is Doing to our Mental Health," Health News, May 8, 2020, available at https://www.healthline.com/health-news/what-covid-19-is-doing-to-our-mental-health.

Katersky, Aaron., "FBI Task Force Focuses on Human Trafficking Amid Coronavirus," ABC News, April 24, 2020, available at https://abcnews.go.com/US/fbi-task-force-focuses-human-trafficking-amid-coronavirus/story?id=70329172.

Kressel, Neil, J., "Mass Hate, The Global Rise of Genocide and Terror", Why People Followed Hitler, Plenum Press, January 24, 2002.

Leuchtenburg, William, E., "Franklin D. Roosevelt: Impact and Legacy," UVA Miller Center, available at https://millercenter.org/president/fdroosevelt/impact-and-legacy.

Levy, Peter, B., "What we Get Wrong about the 1960's Riots," *The Washington Post*, July 21, 2019, available at https://www.washingtonpost.com/outlook/2019/07/21/what-we-get-wrong-about-s-riots/.

Our World Data, "Statistics and Research, Coronavirus Pandemic (Covid-19)," July 22, 2020, available at https://ourworldindata.org/coronavirus.

Peeples, Lynne., "What the Data say about Police Brutality and Racial Bias," A Nature Resource Journal, June 19, 2020, available at https://www.nature.com/articles/d41586-020-01846-z.

Petterson, Steve et al. "Projected Deaths of Despair During the Coronavirus Recession," Well Being Trust, May 8, 2020, WellBeingTrust.org, available at https://wellbeing-trust.org/wp-content/uploads/2020/05/WBT_Deaths-of-Despair_COVID-19-FINAL-FINAL.pdf.

Pew Research Center, Chapter 4., "In a Politically Polarized Era, Sharp Divides in Both Partisan Coalitions" (Washington: 2019), available at https://www.people-press.org/2019/12/17/views-on-race-and-immigration/.

Prison Policy Initiative, "Mass Incarceration: The Whole Pie 2020," March 24, 2020, available at https://www.prisonpolicy.org/reports/pie2020.html.

Redfern, Corinne., "The Pandemic's Hidden Human Trafficking Crisis," *Foreign Policy, April 30, 2020, available at* https://foreignpolicy.com/2020/04/30/coronavirus-pandemic-human-trafficking-crisis/.

Soloman, Danyelle., "Suppression: A Common Thread in American Democracy," Center for American Progress,

June 16, 2017, available at https://www.americanprogress.org/issues/race/news/2017/06/16/434561/suppression-common-thread-american-democracy/.

Tesler, Michael., "The Floyd protests have changed public opinion about race and policing. Here's the data," *The Washington Post*, June 9, 2020, available at https://www.washingtonpost.com/politics/2020/06/09/floyd-protests-have-changed-public-opinion-about-race-policing-heres-data/.

U.S. Bureau of Labor Statistics, "Substance Abuse, Behavioral Disorder and Mental Health Counselors," May 2019, available at https://www.bls.gov/oes/current/oes211018.htm.

Wilson, Jason., "'Cultural Marxism': a uniting theory for right-wingers who love to play the victim," The Guardian, January 18, 2015, available at https://www.theguardian.com/commentisfree/2015/jan/19/cultural-marxism-a-uniting-theory-for-rightwingers-who-love-to-play-the-victim.

World Health Organization, "More than 150 Countries Engaged in Covid-19 Vaccine Global Access Facility," July 15, 2020, available at https://www.who.int/news-room/detail/15-07-2020-more-than-150-countries-engaged-in-covid-19-vaccine-global-access-facility.

Zhu N, Zhang D, Wang W, Li X, Yang B, Song J, et al., "A novel coronavirus from patients with pneumonia in China, 2019," New England Journal of Medicine, 2020, available at https://doi.org/10.1056/NEJMoa2001017.

Made in the USA
Columbia, SC
15 November 2020